Basics of Python Programming

(with computer fundamentals)

By

HARIPRASATH P

HARIPRASATH.P

PREFACE

Writing a book is a not an easy task at all. It requires more magnitude and kind co-operation from many, for its successful completion. I wish to express our sincere thanks to all those who were involved in motivating us to produce this book.

I would like to give our sincere thanks to our honourable **Founder and Chairman, Col. Dr. JEPPIAAR, M.A., B.L., Ph.D.,** for his sincere endeavour in educating us in his premier institution.

I would like to express our deep gratitude to our beloved **Secretary and Correspondent, Dr. P. CHINNADURAI, M.A., M.Phil., Ph.D.,** for his enthusiastic motivation which helped us a lot in completing this book and our sincere thanks to our dynamic **Directors, Mrs. C. VIJAYA RAJESWARI and Mr. C. SAKTHI KUMAR, M.E., M.Phil.,** for providing us with the necessary facilities to complete this book.

I wish to express gratefulness to our **Principal, Dr. K. MANI, M.E., Ph.D.,** for his encouragement and sincere guidance. I wish to convey our special thanks and gratitude to the **Head of the Department, Dr. Mrs. S. MURUGAVALLI, M.E., Ph.D.,** for their encouragement and valuable suggestions without which we would not have completed the book successfully.

HARIPRASATH P

HARIPRASATH.P

My Sincere Thanks
to
My Parents
& to My Department
HOD.

Special Features of this book!

1 This book is very helpful for the beginners to learn about the basic concepts of Python in a deep manner.

2 This book consist of various self-evaluation at the end of each sub-chapters which will increase your learning capacity to a great extend.

3 This book is framed with lot of examples which are very simple and easy to understand.

4 This book is written with simple English so that everyone can understand easily.

5 The possible errors that a beginner can made also discussed effectively throughout this book.

6 Video Tutorials are also available, please visit www.hariprasath.org/python for video tutorials.

7 The Power Point Presentation is also available in my website (www.hariprasath.org/python) which will discuss the concepts briefly in a visual way.

Enjoy Learning!

HARIPRASATH.P

TABLE OF CONTENTS

HARIPRASATH.P

Chapter 01

INTRODUCTION TO PYTHON PROGRAMMING

Chapter 02

BASIC CONCEPTS OF PYTHON
PROGRAMMING

Chapter 03

CONTROL FLOW STATEMENTS IN PYTHON

Chapter 04

DATA STRUCTURES OF PYTHON

⇛ Introduction

⇛ List

⇛ Creation of list

⇛ Operations on list

⇛ Finding the length of list

⇛ Adding contents to the list

⇛ Sorting the list

⇛ Deleting items from list

⇛ Count Method

⇛ Insert Method

⇛ Remove Method

⇛ Pop Method

⇛ Reversing the list

⇛ Copying the items of the list

⇛ Tuples

⇛ Creation of Tuples

⇛ Operations on Tuples

⇛ Dictionaries

⇛ Creation of dictionary

⇛ Adding and deleting Key-Value Pair

HARIPRASATH.P

REVIEW CHAPTER

FUNDAMENTAL CONCEPTS OF COMPUTER SCIENCE

If you can't explain it simply,
You don't understand it well enough!

- Albert Einstein

HARIPRASATH.P

Computer:

Computer is defined as the device which is designed to perform complex operations which takes large amount of time by human to do it. It is an electronic device which works with the help of instructions which are known as programs.

Salient Features of Computers:

Now-a-days computers are used in various fields to carry out various tasks; we are using the computers because of the following salient features of it.

Speed:

Computers need less amount of time to do complex operations. Initially, computers are designed for performing the arithmetic tasks. It is possible by the human to carry out simple calculations in short period. But, computers are capable of calculating the arithmetic complex operations within few seconds. This is the main reason for the popularity of the computers.

Automaticity:

Automaticity is the property of having the capability of starting, operating independently without any instructions by the external environment continuously. It accepts the codes and operates automatically.

Accuracy:

'Creativity is allowing you to make mistakes' – This statement only suits for humans because the computer doesn't do any mistakes during its working. If we give the instructions correctly, it accepts it and performs tasks. Computers are capable of giving nicety results.

Capability of performing variety of skills:

Computers are capable of performing variety of skills in same time. We can able to do various tasks at the same time using computers which are impossible by human. They never confused and thus it shows high versatility.

Storage capacity:

A well-known salient feature of a computer is storage capacity. They are capable of storing large amount of data's. They are having two types of memory such as Primary and Secondary memory. Storage devices like CD's, DVD's, and Pen drives are used to store data's.

Basic Terminologies of Computers:

COMPUTER:

The expansion of computer is 'Commonly Operated Machine Particularly Used for Technical and Educational Research.

Software:

Software is nothing but a group of instructions which are coded using computer languages which helps in instructing the computers to perform the operations.

Hardware:

A physical combination of a computer is said to be hardware. It includes monitor, keyboard, mouse and so on. Generally, computer materials / parts which are able to touch is said to be hardware.

Input Device:

Devices in computers which are used to give input to the computers are said to be input devices. For example, Keyboard is an input device which is helping in giving inputs to the computer by typing.

Output device:

A device which communicates the results of the computer to the outer environment of the computer is framed to be output device. For example, Printer is an output device. The results are obtained as print outs.

HARIPRASATH.P

Bit:

'Bit' is derived from 'BINARY DIGIT' which is the smallest and fundamental unit of computer memory.

Byte:

Combination of eight bits (ie, Binary digits) are said to be bytes.

Storage devices:

Devices which are used for storing data's are said to be storage devices. Without storage devices, computers can't able to store any data. Examples of storage devices are CD, DVD, Zip diskette etc.

Computer language (or)
Programming Language:

A tool or kit which is used to communicate the computer and to control the machine is said to be program. In other words, it is a bunch of instructions which are written with particular rules and regulations in order to communicate the computer system for ordering to perform some operations.

Boot:

This is a process of starting up a computer system. Generally, a start up activity is called as booting.

Shut down:

The process of ending the operating and switching off the computer is said to be shut downing a system.

Saving:

Saving is the process of storing the information in the storage device of the computer. Saving helps to retrieve the document when we need it.

Virus:

Computer virus is types of computer program which reproduce the exact copy of the file another time propagate from one system to another.

Advantages of computers:

1 It reduces our work.

2 A computer reduces our time and energy.

3 They show automaticity and so more advantageous.

4 Computing capacity is high and also shows nicety results.

5 Internet helps to connect the world and shrinks the world.

6 They are helpful in storing large amount of data.

7 Using computers, one can able to re-collect and view the stored date and the modifications can able to do.

8 They are helpful in studies. One can able to learn and acquire large amount of knowledge using PC's.

9 Computers are well known for efficiency and highly efficient.

10 They are widely used in many fields such as industries, business, education, entertainment, banking etc.

Disadvantages of Computers:

Yet we are having large amount of advantages on computers, computer shows some disadvantages and proves the statement 'it is impossible to construct an engine with 100% efficiency'.

1 Internet provides chatting and other some unwanted things which spoil and wastes the time and social life of humans.

2 It may cause, backbone pain and its related disease, if human can do work for large amount of time using PC's.

3 It affects vision.

④ The speed of the computers may slow sometimes and they are little expensive.

⑤ Virus is the big problem which restricts the good condition of computers.

History of Computers:

The following stages explain the invention of computers.

Abacus: (3000 B.C)

① A first manual mechanical device which is invented by Babylon is called abacus.

② It is also called as counting frame and used for performing mathematical operations as particularly addition and subtraction.

③ It is a device made by wood and rods which are easy moving and thus it is used for counting.

John Napier's rod: (1614)

① Napier rods are also a device which is similar to abaci and used for performing the mathematical tasks.

2 Multiplication, division and square root operations are performed using this rod and finding the values are very complex in nature.

3 It consists of wood in which tables are written in a particular design and the calculation is performed using that tables.

4 Later, it was developed as Genaille – Lucas rules which is a new and modified version of Napier rods and it is also arithmetic tool which used to perform arithmetic operations.

Slide Rule: (1622)

1 Slide rule is the advanced mathematical device in olden days which is used to perform multiplication, division and also trigonometric operations.

2 It was invented by William Oughtred and logarithms plays important role in this device.

3 They are designed in many forms such as circular rulers, cylindrical rulers and so on.

❹ Slide ruler technique is difficult to learn and also it may not accurate some time which is a drawback.

Pascal Calculator: (1852)

❶ It is the first arithmetic machine which is invented by Pascal and is a mechanical calculator.

❷ Since it is the first mechanical calculator, it is used for many works and familiar in olden days.

Invention of electricity:

❶ It is important to study about the invention of electricity during the study of invention of PC's because, computer needs electricity to do work.

❷ The flow of charges (electrons) conducts the electricity and the invention of this phenomenon enhances the science in different and advanced direction.

Hollerith Cards:

❶ Punched cards by Hollerith gives the arithmetic information results in form of digital format by the in and out of holes in a pre-defined location.

Electronic Calculator:

❶ After the long period, electronic calculators are invented for performing arithmetic tasks.

❷ It is very small and portable one which can able to perform tasks with less time.

❸ It has buttons, by touching it the calculations can be carried out.

❹ They are capable of running with the help of batteries and solar calculators are introduced now-a-days.

❺ They are very useful and logical operations cannot be performed by using this.

HARIPRASATH.P

Universal Automatic Computer (UNIVAC):

1 UNIVAC consists of vacuum tubes and takes large amount of power supply to do work.

2 It needs large amount of space and not portable and less accurate.

Engines of Charles Babbage:

1 A huge machine which was invented by Charles Babbage for performing operations is said to be difference engine and later it was developed as analytical engine.

2 Analytical engine was coded whereas difference engines are not and analytical engine gives an idea for the invention of computers and so Charles Babbage is called as father of computers.

After the invention of engines by Charles Babbage, memory chips are introduced and then the personal computers are invented which are used widely now-a-days.

HARIPRASATH.P

COMPUTER IS AN ELECTRONIC DEVICE:

Computer is an electronic device. It needs electricity to do work and the components of computer (inside CPU) are made up of semiconductor devices such as IC's and transistors. So, that it is called as an electronic device.

GENERATIONS OF COMPUTER:

Modern computers are the modification of different generation of computers as follows:

First Generation of Computers:

⇒ In 1940's first generation of computers are invented and they are made up of vacuum tubes and resistors.

⇒ For storing data's magnetic drums are used in addition with vacuum tubes.

⇒ ENIAC, EDVAC, EDSAC are some of the examples of first generation of computers.

⇒ ENIAC is the first computer which was made up of vacuum tubes.

⇒ Since there are no languages invented in those years it accepts only binary languages.

⇒ Since vacuum tubes are used, they occupy very large space.

Second Generation of Computers:

⇒ Vacuum tubes are replaced by transistors.

⇒ CDC-3600 is an example for second generation of computers which are having large size.

⇒ Common business oriented language, formula transistor are used.

⇒ They accept low level languages and they are having both input and output devices.

⇒ Magnetic core memory is used for storage.

Third Generation of Computers:

⇒ A type of semiconductor called Integrated Circuits (IC's) is used in this generation of computers.

⇒ Magnetic disks, punched cards are used as devices and it was later replaced because of the invention of printers (dot-matrix)

⇒ 3GL language is used. 3GL language is nothing but a language used in third generation.

HARIPRASATH.P

⇛ The first OS is used in this generation.

⇛SSI technology evolved.

Fourth Generation of Computers:

⇛ Development of Very Large Scale Integration (VLSI) improves the quality of fourth generation of computers.

⇛ Micro-processors and 4GL languages are used in this generation.

⇛ They show excellent speed and more advantageous than any other generations quoted above.

⇛ This is the peak period for the development of computers.

⇛ The rate of computer users increases rapidly during this generation.

Fifth Generation of Computers:

⇛ Human intelligence evaluated in this generation.

⇛ Ability of thinking and reasoning power developed in this generation.

HARIPRASATH.P

⇒ They are faster and top most advantageous, new technology of computers.

⇒ Robots are best examples for this generation of computers.

⇒ Higher level languages like C, C++ are used.

⇒ Super conducting technology is going to be evaluated.

⇒ Powerful, cheaper, compact, portable, thinkable computers are going to evaluate in this generation.

⇒ A robot is an electro-mechanical machine which is controlled by programming is evaluated.

⇒It shows incredible speed and highly efficient.

Classification of Computers:

Computers are classified into many types depends upon the followings:

A) Based on the functionality:

According to this criteria, computers are classified as Analog, digital and hybrid computers.

a) Analog Computers:

Computers which uses physical phenomenon continuously are said to be analog computers. They are fastest computers in olden days.

b) Digital computers:

Computers which are designed to perform calculations and logical operations is said to be digital computers. It releases results in digital format and uses binary numbers.

c) Hybrid Computers:

Combination variety of computers which is obtained from the analog and digital computers are said to be hybrid computers.

B) Based on the size:

a) Super computers:

⇒ Super computers are well known for its speed and it is very expensive in nature.

⇒ They are very larger in size and occupy a room.

HARIPRASATH.P

⇒ They are used in scientific field.

b) Mainframe computers:

⇒ They are also larger and highly efficient in nature.

⇒ It is one of very costlier computers and they are manufactured with multi user facility.

⇒ These computers are having high maintenance cost.

c) Mini Computers:

⇒ When compared with the mainframe computers, small computers are said to be mini computers.

⇒ As the name implies, they are very smaller and shows good salient features.

⇒ They provide high speed and efficiency and speed of the mini computer is about one and fifty million instruction per second.

⇒ It is note-worthy than that of the main frame computers.

d) Micro computers:

⇒ A larger computer which occupies a whole room is replaced by a small single circuit chip and it is said to be micro computer.

⇒ They are more advantageous when compared with the other classification of computers since they are having some special features like small in size, highly portable and cost is very less.

TABLE: – CLASSIFICATION OF COMPUTERS – EXAMPLES

Classification of Computer	Example	Application
Micro computers	Notebooks, desktops	Used in industrial, educational purposes and as well as entertainment.
Mini Computers	IBM	Used for industrial as well as research.
Main frame computers	ICL	Designed for industrial purpose.
Super computers	Cray Super computers	Designed to increase the efficiency and used in scientific applications

C) Classification of Personal Computers:

PC's / Personal Computers are classified as follows,

a) Desktop:

A computer which is widely used now-a-days which consists of CPU as its heart is said to be desktop computer. It comprises the parts such as keyboard, mouse, monitor and so on.

b) Laptop:

Portable form for desktop is said to be laptop computer. They are portable and it occupy small place even lap is enough.

c) Touch screen computers:

Touch screen technology is rapidly developed now-a-days. Touch screen computers consists of monitor in which the operations are performed by touching the screen. They are also called as Palmtops.

Palmtops technologies are emerging the world now-a-days.

HARIPRASATH.P

DIFFERENCES BETWEEN DESKTOP AND LAPTOP:

SI.NO	Desktop's	Laptops
1.	They are non-portable	They are non-portable.
2.	They are not capable for storing electrical energy and retrieving it without the help of devices like UPS.	They are capable of storing electrical energy via batteries.
3.	Batteries are not used for the storage of energy.	Lithium battery is used

DEVICES:

a) INPUT DEVICES:

Devices which are useful for giving the inputs to the computer system are said to be input devices.

1. KEYBOARD:

Keyboard is the most common input device which gives the data to the computers. It is a typing device in which the letters, numbers, symbols are printed in it. With the help of these, one can able to send the data to the computers.

Types of Keyboard:
1. Standard keyboards:

Standard keyboards are having the keys such as alphabetic, numeric, function and symbol keys and it has the standard dimension.

2. Note book sized:

Keyboards which are available for the laptops and having compressed set of keys are said to be note book sized keyboards.

Note: *In a standard keyboard 104 keys are available.*

Types of Keys in keyboard:
Alpha numeric keys:

Alpha refers alphabetic letters ranges from A to Z and numeric refers numbers 0 to 9. The set

HARIPRASATH.P

of alphabetic letters and number keys are said to be alpha numeric keys.

Punctuation keys:

The keys which are used for putting the punctuations such as semicolons (;), Brackets (), Symbols (+ , - , * , /) are said to be punctuation keys.

Arrow keys:

Up, down, left and right arrows are available in the keyboard which is termed as arrow keys and they are used to move the position of the window from one region to another.

Delete Key:

A single key in the keyboard which is printed as 'Del' is said to be delete key and the major use of the key is deleting something whether it may be a file, folder and so on.

Enter key:

A key which is used for executing the entering process is said to be enter key. This plays a vital role in the keys of keyboard.

Function keys:

Keys which are designed to perform particular set of special functions is said to be function keys. It is printed as F1 to F12.

Escape key:

It is the exit key which is used for closing the task or disconnecting the operation immediately.

Control Key:

Ctrl keys are used for controlling some operations. It varies from one program to another. For example, in Ms-Word window, if we press Ctrl + B, it prints the text in bold letter. (Control of the letter is activated as bold)

Backspace key:

It is just used for erasing the last character from the position of the mouse.

Alternate Key (Alt):

It is special type of key which is used as alternate keys in some situations. If we press Alt + F4, the program terminates.

Caps lock:

It is used to change the case of text as upper as well as lower cases. Example: Upper case: WELCOME, Lower case: Welcome

Page up and Page down:

It is generally used to visualize the pages as per our recruitment.

Print screen:

It is used to print the specific screen which is active at the time. One can able to print the screen by pressing this key.

Tab:

It is used for alignment of texts and moving the position of the cursor.

General Keyboard shortcuts:

S.NO	Shortcut	Application
1.	Ctrl + A	Select all
2.	Shift + Delete	Permanent deletion
3.	Delete	Temporary deletion
4.	F2	Renaming the selecting file
5.	F3	Searching the folder
6.	Alt + Enter	Shows the features of the items
7.	Alt + F4	Ending program
8.	Ctrl + Esc	Display start menu
9.	Ctrl + Tab	Viewing multiple tasks
10.	F1	For help
11.	Ctrl + P	Printing a file
12.	Print screen	Printing the screen
13.	F5	Refreshing

HARIPRASATH.P

14.	Alt + Spacebar	Shows the menu of the window
15.	Delete	Used for deletion purpose

2. Mouse:

Mouse is a commonly used pointing input device. It has different functions and three major buttons.

Types:

1. Optical mouse:

Light emitting diode (LED) technology is evolved in this type of mouse

2. Coherent mouse:

Mouse which is using laser light technology is said to be coherent or laser mouse.

3. Mouse for games:

Mouse which is discovered for playing games are said to be gaming mouse.

HARIPRASATH.P

4. Stress fewer mice:

Mouse which is designed for good style of manufacturing and less stressful while using it for long time is said to stress fewer mice.

5. Wireless mouse:

Now-a-days wireless mouse is used widely. They are comfort, portable, highly sensitive in nature. USB's and blue tooth are used for functioning of wireless mouse.

6. Mechanical:

Mechanical sensors are used and rubber balls are connected.

7. Opt-mechanical:

In addition to mechanical sensors, optical sensors are evaluated in these types of mouse.

Other some input devices:

a) Bar code reader:

It used for reading the barcodes which are printed. This device is widely used in many places now.

b) Scanner:

The device which is used to scan some files and saving it into the computer system is said to be a scanner. In other words, it is a device which is used to take the copy of the one particular file and used to store in it inside the computer. These are the some of the examples of input devices.

OUTPUT DEVICES:

Devices which are designed for obtaining outputs are said to be output device. Printer is a general output device.

Printer:

Printer is a device which is used to take print outs. There are many types of printers available now-a-days such as dot-matrix, laser, ink-jet and so on.

LASER PRINTER:

Laser printer provides the excellent quality of printing. Photo-conductivity phenomenon is evaluated in this printer for printing the file.

HARIPRASATH.P

LED PRINTER:

Printers which are using the Light Emitting diode (LED) technology are said to be LED printers. They are more efficient and give quality printout when compared with laser printers.

INK JET PRINTERS:

A small sized inexpensive, cheaper printers which are used to take print outs for simple purposes are said to be ink jet printers. They are capable of giving effective printing.

BIOLOGICAL HAZARDS OF PRINTERS:

1. A toner particle which is smaller and present inside the printer causes the health injuries such as lung diseases.

2. Powders are used in toners are not eco-friendly.

3. Probability of respiratory disease and increase in pollution will be high because of using printers.

HARIPRASATH.P

4. It may cause cardio-vascular problems since it has ultrafine particles.

MONITORS:

Monitor is a device which is used for converting the machine code to human understandable format. (ie, it is an output device)

Types:

1. CRT Monitors:

Cathode ray tubes are used in this monitors. They are highly big in size when compared to other types and also huge in weight and so power consumption is very high.

2. LCD Monitors:

Liquid crystal display technology is evolved in this type of monitors. As compared to CRT, it is more advantageous.

3. Plasma Monitors:

Plasma discharge technology is used and it is well known for its special features like good aspect ratio and it doesn't allow the external devices (say light pens) which is a drawback.

DIFFERENCES BETWEEN CRT AND LCD MONITORS:

S.NO	CRT MONITORS	LCD MONITORS
1.	Larger in size	Smaller in size
2.	Consumes large energy	Consumes less energy
3.	Cathode ray tubes used	Liquid crystal display phenomenon used

HAZARDS OF MONITORS:

1. Light rays from the monitor affect our eye and causes vision problems.

2. It emits electromagnetic radiations which affects our body as well as environment.

PRECAUTION MEASURES:

1. Don't work with computers overall a day and take a break for sometimes to relax your eyes.

2. Ensure the light intensity of the monitor is in correct ratio.

HARIPRASATH.P

3. Use the screen filters which restricts the radiations.

4. Maintain a specific distance between your eye and PC.

Computers use different display technologies such as CRT's, LCD's, and LED's and so on

CRT Display:

CRT stands for Cathode Ray tube display which is a type of monitor display.

Principle of CRT display:

The CRT works on the following principles

1. Thermionic emission which defines the heat induced flow of charge carriers from a surface.

2. Electron beam deflection which occurs due to electric and magnetic field.

3. Production of fluorescence by electron beam.

HARIPRASATH.P

Parts of CRT:

a) Electron Gun:

It is used for the production of electrons and the process called thermionic emission is used for producing the electrons and the electrons produced are having very high speed and velocity. Electrons produced are passes over the different series of control grids which controls the contrast of the image.

b) Deflection system:

For controlling the image produced the deflection system is used.

c) Fluorescent screen:

For displaying the hitting of electrons it is used. I was coated by the material like phosphorous which reflects light when electron strikes.

Working of CRT:

It contains large amount of small red, green, blue colored dots. The colored dots undergo glowing when it was stricken by the electron beams which travel across the screen and thus it creates image. The electrons are negatively charged and the screen gives the positive charge and so the screen glows and produces the image.

Applications:

1. It is used in televisions, monitors.

2. CRT's are used in Cathode Ray Oscilloscopes

Advantages of CRT:

1. Highly colorful one and so produces more colors.

2. Cheaper in nature.

3. Quality of the image displayed by CRT monitors is very good.

4. They allow light guns.

Disadvantages of CRT:

1. Requires high voltage for working.

2. CRT causes health effects such as eye problems in humans.

3. They are larger in size and uses very big screen display.

4. Flickers may produced.

Biological Hazards of CRT's:

1. Rays emitted are harmful to human body as well as environment.

2. Requires high charge and so the energy gets wasted.

3. They emits electromagnetic radiations which are harmful

4. They are manufactured from leaded gas and so harmful to environment.

b) Liquid Crystal Display (LCD)
Principle:

The light passes through the liquid crystal (ie, inter lying substance in between solid and liquid state), when it is stimulated by a charge is the basic principle of LCD display.

Working:

It consists of large amount of smaller segments called pixels. It consist of electrode and polarizer. The light is allowed to pass through the polarizer and so when the voltage is applied then electrodes control the liquid crystal orientation.

Thus it changes the level of illumination in each pixel and produces the image. Electrodes produce the field which alternates the crystal, which lines the light up with the polarizing filter and allows it to pass through it.

Applications of LCD's:

1. In calculators, LCD displays are widely used.

2. It is also used in computer display.

3. Televisions, camera's uses this LCD's.

Advantages of LCD's:

1. Flat screens are produced using LCD.

2. Flickering is comparatively less.

3. Geometric distortion is less.

4. Heat emission and power consumption is very less comparatively.

5. Available in different sizes and shapes.

Disadvantages:

1. They are not cheaper one and it is very costlier comparatively.

HARIPRASATH.P

2. It is unable to change the resolution display in LCD and it is allotted as constant one.

c) LED Display: (Light Emitting Diode)
Principle:

LED is a device which converts electrical to light energy. LED is a semiconductor material which emits the light (monochromatic) when it is forward biased.

Working:

When voltage is given to the chip (LED is nothing but a semiconductor chip), electrons flow takes place. In the n-part it has capable energy to move across p-junction. During the recombination process, energy is emitted in form of photon of light.

Applications of LED's:

1. In bar code reader, mobiles, laptops.

2. Digital camera's uses LED.

3. They are used in traffic signals and general lighting.

Advantages:

⇛ Life period is very high.

⇛ They show good efficiency.

⇛ They are smaller in size.

⇛ They didn't emit harmful rays.

Disadvantages:

⇛Cost is very high.

MEMORY AND ITS TYPES:

Computer memory is classified as volatile and non – volatile.

1. Volatile memory:

Memory which becomes dead when the power is gets off is said to be volatile memory. Example: RAM (Random Access Memory) There is two types of RAM namely DRAM (Dynamic Random Access Memory) and SRAM (Static random access memory)

2. Non-Volatile memory:

The memory which doesn't need power to alive is said to be non-volatile memory. Examples are ROM (Read Only Memory), floppy disks and so on.

These are the two basic classification of memory.

FUNCTIONING MECHANISM OF A COMPUTER SYSTEM TO CARRY OUT TASKS:

As we discussed already, input, output and storage devices plays vital role in the activation of the hardware by software (ie, functioning of a computer system)

Step: 1 *Gathering information's via input device:*

1. For performing any task, computers should need some amount of data and the data was captured by the help of input devices.

2. Keyboard is the most common input device and using that device computer acquires the data from the user.

3. Thus, computers gather the information and made ready for the process.

Step: 2   *Processing the operations inside the CPU:*

1. After getting the input, the computer undergoes processing.

2. CPU is the major part which helps on processing the data.

3. The order of instructions is instructed by the control unit.

4. If any arithmetic operations are instructed by the user, then the control is given to the arithmetic logical unit.

5. ALU helps in performing the arithmetic and logical tasks.

Thus the required operation was performed by the units of CPU.

Step: 3   *Storing the output:*

1. After finishing the process, computers stores the result in storage devices either it may be primary or secondary storage devices.

2. Informations may be stored using storage devices like CD's.

HARIPRASATH.P

Step: 4   *Generalizing output:*

1. After the storage process, computer announces the output or the result of the task performed by it.

2. Output devices like printers are used for the displaying the outputs.

Thus, by capturing the input via input device and processing the data by various units inside the central processing unit, computer shows the result / output via output devices. This is said to be functioning mechanism of computer system.

CPU IS CALLED AS HEART OF COMPUTER:

In the mechanism of functioning of a computer system, several sequences are controlled by the CPU and also CPU helps in instructing the flow of the task. Hence it is called as Heart of the computers.

APPLICATIONS OF COMPUTERS IN VARIOUS FIELDS:

a) Medical field:

1. In medical field, it is used for diagnostic purpose of diseases.

2. In echocardiography, computers play an active role.

3. For taking X-rays, CT scans computers are widely used.

4. Computers are used to store the details of the patients.

5. Magnetic Resonance Imaging (MRI) is possible with the help of computers.

6. It is used to view the internal parts of the organs.

7. It is widely used in the time of surgery.

8. It helps in medical research.

9. Computers help in storing and finding the Blood pressure, oxygen levels etc.

10. They are also used for billing purpose in hospitals.

HARIPRASATH.P

b) Entertainment:

1. Computers are well-known entertainers. With the help of internet connection one can download videos, songs etc.

2. Chatting with friends is also possible using computers.

3. Computers are used to play games.

4. They are used in making animations, cartoons etc.

5. Editing photos, videos are also possible.

6. One can able to spend their time by studying books, magazines via net using computers.

c) Education:

1. Online library helps to improve the knowledge of students.

2. Internet provides lot of good information to the students.

3. e-learning is also possible.

4. For storing the details of the students, it is used in educational institutions.

HARIPRASATH.P

⑤ Computer education helps to improve the talent of the students.

d) Banks:

❶ For saving the details of the accounts, computers are widely used in banks.

❷ Calculations are carried out with the computers in banking which reduces the time and highly accurate and efficient.

❸ For watching the banks, computers are used with the help of web camera.

e) Other applications:

❶ For booking tickets for cinema, travelling and so on.

❷ To generate 2D and 3D animations.

❸ For printing purposes.

❹ To do mathematical tasks.

❺ In billing purpose in various places like medical shops, shopping centers and so on.

These are the some of the applications of computers.

Battery used in laptops – LITHIUM ION BATTERY:

Laptop's uses Lithium ion battery for storing the charge. LIB is a rechargeable battery. The charge / discharging efficiency of LIB battery is about 80-90%.

Shapes of LIB:

⇒ Cylindrical in shape – Used in laptop's

⇒ Soft, flat, pouch shaped – Used in mobile phones.

Advantages of LIB:

⇒Less in weight and portable.

⇒ Rechargeable in nature.

⇒ Self – discharging rate is lesser.

⇒ Available in different size.

Disadvantages of Lithium Ion Batteries:

❶Protection is needed.

OPERATING SYSTEM

Operating system is nothing but software (System) which executes the hardware or which makes the hardware to do work. Some of the operating system widely used now-a-days are Windows 7, Windows XP, and Vista and so on.

Salient features / Purpose of Operating System:

❶It increases the efficiency of the system.

❷It makes the hardware to execute.

❸It plays vital role in performing tasks.

Generations of Operating System:

First Generation of Operating System:

In first generation, machines never use operating system. They are manual. So that, operating system not required and also no programming languages too. However, vacuum tubes and plug board technologies used.

Second Generation of Operating System:

Transistors and batch systems used. Batch system is used to control the system.

Third Generation of Operating System:

IC's and multiprogramming concept introduced. Multiprogramming is nothing but the execution of many programs in a system simultaneously. In this system, in addition to this, Spooling concept is invented. Spooling is the acronym of Simultaneous Peripheral operations online.

Fourth Generation of Operating System:

LSI (Large Scale Integration Chips) and VLSI (Very Large Scale Integration) revolves the world now-a-days.

TYPES OF SEMICONDUCTOR MEMORY:
RANDOM ACCESS MEMORY (RAM):

RAM is an example for semiconductor storage device.

Types:

❶ Static RAM (SRAM)

❷ Dynamic RAM (DRAM)

❸ Phase change memory (PRAM)

Static RAM: (SRAM)

❶ It consists of 6 MOSFET's (Metal oxide semiconductor field effect transistor) and 4 transistors

❷ They stores binary bits (0's and 1's)

3 It is faster and efficient. Accessing time is 9-10 nano seconds.

Dynamic RAM: (DRAM)

1 They use capacitors and IC's.

2 It uses one capacitor and transistor per bit and so it is very smaller.

READ ONLY MEMORY: (ROM):

Types:

⇒ Programmable Read only memory (PROM)

⇒ Erasable Programmable Read only memory (EPROM)

⇒ Electrically erasable programmable read only memory (EEPROM)

PROM:

⇒ It is designed by using PROM Programmer.

⇒ It also takes binary values.

EPROM:

⇒ PROM is unable to erase but EPROM can be erasable memory.

⇒ If we place EPROM in UV light it gets erased.

⇒ It consists of field-effect transistor.

EEPROM:

⇒ They are used to store small data.

⇒ This memory is erasable when we expose it into electrical field.

Computer Organization

Generally, we know that the computer is an electronic device which consists of collective combination of various physical units so called hardware and the software which is a set of coding makes the hardware to work and the operating system will serves as a platform for the software and as well as the hardware.

For any operation to be performed by the computer, the pre-conditions should be advertised to the computer, such things are generally known as input to the computer, in order to process the input, a processing unit should be available, such unit is said to be "brain of the computer" (Central Processing Unit). After processing operation, there are two possibilities exists.,

HARIPRASATH.P

❶ The processed result so called output may be stored into any memory units.

❷ The second case is that, the output may be thrown to user terminal without saving it internally.

Hence, these basic operations will give a sketch to the basic computer organization.

Basic Computer Organization:

The following diagram (Fig: 1.1) illustrates the basic computer organization and it comprises of various units that are connected via the bus. Hence, before discussing the basic computer organization it is very essential to have an idea about the basic concepts of bus.

Bus:

In computer science terminology, bus is a communicator (or) we can say it as a system which consists of collection of wires and used for transferring the messages inside the system. The messages can be transmitted between the devices of the system. The message transfer operation may be of two different categories. They are,

❶ Unidirectional Message Transfer

❷ Bi-directional Message Transfer

In case of unidirectional message transfer, the data will be transferred in one way and such buses are called as unidirectional buses, whereas some buses with transfer data to and fro (bi-directionally) such buses are called as bidirectional buses.

Some of the common examples for the bus include PCI, SCSI and USB.

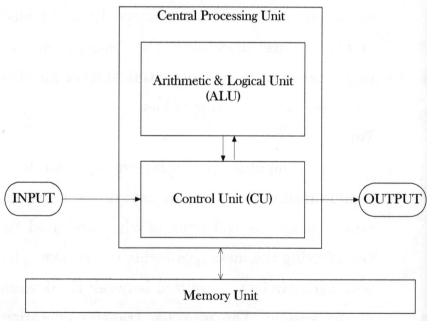

Figure 1.1. : Basic Computer Organization

Input and Output Units:

In the schematic diagram of basic computer organization, both input as well as output units are responsible for getting the input (via input device) and displaying the output (via output device).

Memory Unit:

After processing the data, the data must be stored into some units, such units are said to be memory unit. The memory which is associated with CPU are often called as main memory.

If the main memory is full, some information is moved into the secondary devices (like floppy, USB flash drives) and such things are called as secondary memory. In addition to the concept of main memory and secondary memory we have a special sort of memory called as cache memory.

If a processor requests a data item X, it should be fetched from the main memory. Accessing the main memory will increases time complexity, in order to overcome such drawbacks, the intermediate memory called as "cache memory" is used. The further explanations of cache memory will be discussed in the upcoming chapters.

Central Processing Unit: (CPU)

In the schematic diagram, the central processing unit is divided into two separate sections as control unit and arithmetic logic unit (ALU). The control unit is responsible for getting the input from the user via the input devices and after receiving the input, the control unit will parses the input, if the operation to be performed has any *arithmetic or logical operations* in such cases, it will transfer the control to the ALU unit. The ALU is responsible for performing such operations and afterwards, it returns the control to the control unit again. After operation was performed, the control unit may save the result into memory or directly throws the result to the output terminal. If CPU receives data from memory such operation is called as READ operation and the vice versa is called as WRITE operation.

Thus the basic computer organization performs the operations with the help of above devices.

Computer Architecture:

After learning about the basic computer organization, we can easily coin the definition for Computer Architecture, that is, Computer Architecture is the study of design and logic of the computer system. It gives an idea about how the computer system was designed and how they are logically connected with one another.

In basic computer organization, we discussed how the various devices are connected in such a way to perform operations effectively. Major operations are executed by the CPU. The Central Processing Unit uses instruction sets.

Assembly Language Program:

The major area of computer architecture deals with CPU. The processing unit uses the

Assembly languages which consist of set of instruction sets.

Instruction Set:

Instruction set consists of various set of commands that are readily available for execution by the CPU. As the name implies, it instructs CPU regarding what operation is to be performed. The need of instruction set is to instruct the CPU regards what operations to be performed and how data is to be fetched.

Why to go for Assembly Language?

High level languages are not understandable form of languages by the system and they are understandable by the compiler which means the compiler is system software that takes high level language as input and converts it to Assembly language (or) any other target code. The Assembly language will be converted into machine codes by the system architecture. The machine codes are not understandable by the human but can be understandable by the user. Hence, in computer architecture the study of Assembly language is very essential.

Opcode and Operands:

An assembly language will consist of set of mnemonics which has opcode and operands. The Opcode (operational code) which defines what operation is to be performed. (MOV – which refers data movement operation) and operand describes on which data the operation is to be performed.

For better understanding, refer the example (Figure 1.2) given below which performs the addition of two numbers using ALP and Figure 1.3 has the description for the code.

MVI A,#02	#Line 1
MOV B,A	#Line 2
MVI C,#02	#Line 3
ADD C,B	#Line 4

Figure 1.2: ALP for Addition

Explanation:

Description:

1. MVI - Move Immediately, Consider that the syntax is of [MVI Destination, Source], Hence the data (immediate data) 02 is moved to Accumulator.

2. In this line, the content(A) i.e. 2 is moved to B. Hence Mem(B) has the value 2.

3. Here, the operation performed gives result as Mem(C)=2.

4. C holds result: C=B+C (C already holds 2, and B was already loaded with 2, hence C holds the result as 4)

Figure 1.3: Description for ALP given in the Fig: 1.2

Thus, the CPU gets such sort of ALP coding and it will generate the machine codes which consist of 0's and 1's which cannot be understandable by the human.

General Types of Instructions:

Instruction Sets varies from processor to processor. In computer architecture, we can frame some general instruction set for a hypothetical machine for better understanding.

1. Load   -   Loads the Data

HARIPRASATH.P

2. Add   -   Perform   Addition
   Operation on data
3. Store   -   Stores the result / data
   into memory or register.
4. Sub   -   Subtracting Operation.

The above figure shows an introductory view to general instruction sets. There are various types of instructions exists. They are,

Load and Store Instructions:

These instructions are used for moving the data between registers and memory. Example : Load A, Store B.

Arithmetic Instructions:

These instructions are used to perform arithmetic operations like addition, subtraction, multiplication etc. Example: ADD B,C.

Logical Instructions:

Logical   Instructions   are   used   for performing the logical operations like OR, AND etc. Example : ANI (AND operation with immediate data in 8085 Architecture)

Jumping Instructions:

It is used for jumping from one memory location to another. The Jump may be of conditional or unconditional jumps. In case of conditional jump, the jump occurs whenever a condition meets. In unconditional, if such statement executed itself, the jumping will occur immediately. Example: In 8085 Machine Architecture, J 2046 refers, jumping to memory location 2046 immediately without checking any condition (unconditional jump) whereas instruction JNZ 2155 refers to conditional jump, (jump on non-zero)

Control Instructions:

These instructions are used for the purpose of controlling and coordinating tasks. Examples are

⇒ *NOP* – No Operation Performed.

⇒ *HLT* – Halt instruction, which stops execution suddenly.

⇒ *DI, EI* – Disabling and Enabling Interrupts.

Processor Execution Cycle: (PEC)

In the basic computer organization, we have studied how any task will be carried out by the computer. The control unit will get the mnemonic and finds equivalent machine code, and then executes the operation also. In this section, we will discuss how processor will internally work.

The following figure 1.4 illustrates the Processor Execution Cycle.

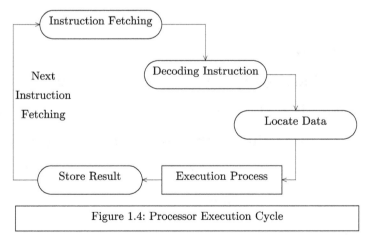

Figure 1.4: Processor Execution Cycle

The above figure illustrates five stages for execution of an instruction by a processor.

Instruction Fetching:

It is process of getting the instruction. The instructions will be obtained in this phase. The Program Counter is the register which holds address of next instruction that has to be executed.

Decoding Instruction:

Decoding instruction is the activity in which the fetched instruction will be examined in order to find its size and identifying machine code of an instruction also performed in this stage.

Locate Data:

Identifying where the data is available for performing the operations. The data may be available readily in the instruction itself (in case of immediate instruction) or it may be available in register or memory.

Execution Process:

Execution process refers to the task of performing operation with the fetched data. The main activity (processing) is performed in this stage. This stage may refers ALU if the instruction as any arithmetic or logical operation.

Store Result:

Store result is the activity by which the result has been stored to memory location or registers for future usage. After storing operation, the next instruction will be fetched with the help of the program counter and hence the cycle gets repeated.

Architectural Models:

In this section, we will discuss some different types of Computer Architecture Models that are available.

Von Neumann Architecture:

The Von Neumann Architecture is nothing but the architecture of the basic computer organization. Refer the section 1.2 for further

HARIPRASATH.P

explanations about the Von Neumann Architecture.

RISC Architecture:

⇒ It is a microprocessor based architecture

⇒ It refers Reduced Instruction Set Computer.

⇒ As the name implies, it has less instructions and very constrained addressing modes.

⇒ It relatively uses very large number of registers.

CISC Architecture:

⇒ CISC refers to Complex Instruction Set Computer.

⇒ It is also microprocessor based architecture.

⇒ CISC has large set of instructions.

⇒ Intel Pentium Processors are the example for CISC architecture.

⇒ This architecture provides high regularity and also uses very less number of registers.

Instruction Set Architecture: (ISA)

The instruction set architecture consists of computer architecture that is related to the programming and which allows different computer types with same ISA to run identical software. The deals with memory organization, registers and instruction sets.

It includes 3-different types of ISA architecture. They are,

1. Stack Architecture
2. Accumulator Architecture
3. General Purpose Register Architecture.

Stack Architecture:

As the name implies, the stack architecture uses the stack data structure. Stack ADT follows the LIFO (Last In First Out) concept in which it uses two primary operations push and pop. The push operation is used for inserting the data and pop is used for removing the data from the stack.

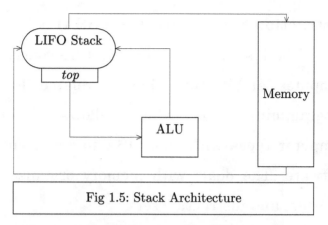

Fig 1.5: Stack Architecture

The above figure illustrates the stack architecture in which LIFO stack has been used. In order to perform operation, the operands are push and operation will be performed. For example: $A = M + N$ has the following steps,

(1) Push M

(2) Push N

(3) Add

(4) Pop A

The advantage of stack architecture is that it has very limited sort of instructions and hence it is easy to write the coding and the drawback of this architecture is the usage of stack which is ineffective in case of longer operations.

Note that: Top of the stack is accessed in order to push and pop the data. Top pointer gets increased to push and decremented to pop out the data from the stack. Java Virtual Machines (JVM) uses the stack architecture.

Accumulator Architecture:

Before discussing about the concept of accumulator architecture, we have to coin the definition for accumulator. The accumulator is a special register which is used for storing the results of arithmetic and logical operations result immediately. The Computer Architecture model which uses the accumulator is said to be "accumulator architecture". The schematic sketch of accumulator architecture is shown in the figure given below (Figure: 1.7)

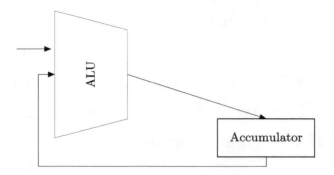

Figure 1.7.: Accumulator Architecture

Example:

Consider the following example of executing the instruction $A=M+N$, in which the sequence of steps are

(1) Load M

(2) Add N

(3) Store A.

We can easily identify the difference between stack architecture and accumulator based architecture. In stack architecture, push and pop are the two operations used and it may increase the complexity, but in case of accumulator based architecture. The immediate result is stored into the accumulator. Hence, no of instructions relatively reduced in this architecture model.

General Purpose Register Architecture:

General Purpose Register Architecture is classified into three different categories. They are,

⇒ Register – Memory Architecture.

⇒ Register – Register Architecture

⇒ Memory – Memory Architecture.

Register – Memory Architecture:

Register Memory Architecture includes operands one for source and another one for the destination in which, one of it is a register and another one is a memory. The general syntax of Register – Memory Architecture is

$[opcode\_specification \quad destination, source]$ In which destination/source may be of register or memory which is expressed as

$$destination \: / \: source = \begin{cases} register(R_0...R_n) \\ Memory(A, B, C..) \end{cases}.$$

The architecture of the R – M will consist of ALU, register and memory. The input to the ALU is register and memory.

Example:

Consider the example *K=M+N,* for this expression evaluation the operational sequence code (the ALP code) for R – M Architecture is given by,

(1)   Load R0, M

(2)   Add R0, N

(3)   Store K, R0

Note: The source and destination may be varied in various architectures. We can assume the Source and Destination fields as of format,

$[opcode\_specification \qquad destination, source]$

throughout this book.

The following diagram (Figure 1.8) will illustrates the R – M Architecture,

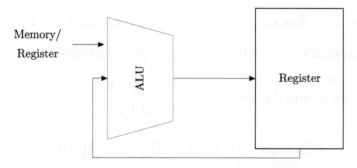

Figure 1.8: Register - Memory Architecture

HARIPRASATH.P

Register – Register Architecture:

Register – Register Architecture is also called as Load and Store Architecture which is used to allow memory that has to be accessed by load and store operations. The operands are loaded from memory and stored in the register. Example: $A = M + N$ can be expressed as,

(1)   Load R0, M.

(2)   Load R1, N.

(3)   Add R0, R1

(4)   Store A, R0

Similarly you can easily frame out the concepts of the M – M Architecture.

Computer Arithmetic:

The arithmetic operations and logical operations are carried out by the ALU unit. Hence, this section (Computer Arithmetic) deals with the study of designing the ALU. The ALU performs arithmetic operations like addition, subtraction, multiplication and division. Similarly it performs logical operations like AND,

OR etc. ALU uses hardware for performing such operation. This topic will help you to understand some concepts about ALU design.

Logical Gates:

The logical is a basic part of digital circuit. ALU circuit comprises of various logical gates that are connected in such a way to perform effective and relevant operations. The basic logic gates includes OR, AND, NOT, NAND, NOR, EX-OR and EX-NOR. The following table illustrates the truth table and symbol of such logical gates.

Note that, the logical gates will work on binary values, *Binary Value*= $\begin{cases} 0, low \\ 1, high \end{cases}$

Name of the Gate	Symbol	Description	Truth Table		
OR Gate $(A+B)$		Has High output if any one of the input is high, else low.	A	B	*Output*
			0	0	0
			0	1	1
			1	0	1
			1	1	1

AND Gate (AB)		Stimulates High output if both of the input is high, It has low output for any other cases.	A	B	*Output*
			0	0	0
			0	1	0
			1	0	0
			1	1	1
NOT Gate $\overline{x}$ x' $\sim x$		It complements the input	I/P	Output	
			0	1	
			1	0	
NOR Gate		Stimulates High output if both of the input is low. (ULG)	A	B	*Output*
			0	0	1
			1	0	0
			0	1	0
			1	1	0

NAND Gate		Stimulates low output if both the inputs are high in all other cases the output is high. It is also called universal logic gate	A	B	Output
			0	0	1
			0	1	1
			1	0	1
			1	1	0

EX-OR Gate $x \oplus y$		It produces low output if the inputs are same	A	B	Output
			0	0	0
			0	1	1
			1	0	1
			1	1	0

EX-NOR Gate $\overline{x \oplus y}$		It produces high output if the inputs are same	A	B	Output
			0	0	1
			0	1	0
			1	0	0
			1	1	1

The above shown table lists the various logic gates which are acting as a basic element for designing the logical circuit in ALU. To design a good and effective logic circuit the study of Boolean algebra is essential.

Boolean Algebra:

Let us initially start with how to draw the logic circuit for the given Boolean expression. Consider the Boolean expression as $x = (A+B)(B'+C)$. The + operations are drawn with OR gate, the inverting operations (Eg: C' or $\overline{C}$) are implemented with NOT gate, '.' Operations are implemented with the AND Gate as shown in the figure given below.

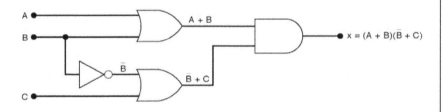

Figure: 1.9: Circuit Diagram for $x = (A+B)(B'+C)$

HARIPRASATH.P

Laws for the Simplification of Boolean Expressions:

To reduce the number of gates in the circuit, makes the hardware to be faster and also avoid complexity in design. In order to reduce the circuit without affecting its original nature, the proper simplification rules has to be applied on it. Some of the rules for reducing / simplifying expressions as follows,

Name of Law/Rule	AND Implementation	OR Implementation
Identity law	$1X = X$	$0+X = X$
Dominance Law	$0X = 0$	$1 + X = 1$
Idempotent law	$XX=X$	$X+X=X$
Inverse law	$XX' = 0$	$X+X' = 1$
Commutative law	$XY=YX$	$X+Y=Y+X$
Associative law	$X(YZ)=(XY)Z$	$(X+Y)+Z=X+(Y+Z)$

Distributive law	$X+YZ=(X+Y)(X+Z)$	$X(Y+Z)=XY+XZ$
Double Negation	$(xx')=x$	--
De Morgan's law	$(xy)'=x'+y'$	$(x+y)'=x'y'$

Example 1: Simplify the Boolean Expression: $T =$ AB+A(B+C).

Solution:

$T = AB + A(B+C)$

(Given)

$T = AB + AB + AC$

(Distributive law)

$T = AB + AC$

(Idempotent law)

which is the simplified Boolean expression which cannot be further simplified.

Example 2: Simplify the Boolean Expression:

$X = A'B + AB + AA' + AB' + AC + BC + CA + ABB$

Solution:

$X = A'B + AB + AA' + AB' + AC + BC + CA + ABB$

$X = A'B + AB + 0 + AB' + AC + BC + CA + AB$

$X = B(A' + A) + AB' + AB + AC + BC + CA$

$X = B(1) + A(B+B') + AC + BC + CA$

$X = B + A(1) + AC + AC + BC$

$X = B + A + AC + BC$

$X = B + A(1+C) + BC$

$X = B + A(1) + BC$

$X = B + A + BC$

$X = B + BC + A$

$X = B(1+C) + A$

$X = B + A$

$X = A + B$ which is the simplified expression.

Design of Arithmetic Circuits:

Half Adder:

Consider a situation of adding two single digit binary numbers. We already familiar with that binary numbers takes only two values [0,1]. Hence for addition, four combination invokes. They are,

(0+0), (0+1), (1+0) and (1+1) the output of (0+0=0, 1+0=1, 0+1=1) whereas the output of (1+1=10) hence it will make a carry of '1'. For more convenience we will make 0's in before of the above resultant, hence the modified resultant is of (0+0=00, 1+0=01, 0+1=10,1+1=10). Hence the truth table is of,

A	B	Carry	Sum
0	0	0	0
0	1	0	1
1	0	0	1
1	1	1	0

Figure: 1.11 – Half Adder Truth Table

If you notice the above table, we can easily find that carry gives output of *AND* gate and *SUM* gives the output of EX-OR Gate. Hence, we can derive circuit for half-adder as

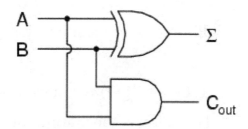

Figure: 1.12 – Half Adder Circuit

Design of Full Adder:

Consider the addition of 3 single digit binaries; in this case we need to have 3 input lines. Here the line – 3 will acts as a carry. We can easily understand the full-adder by the help of diagram given below,

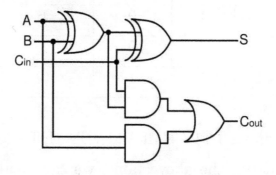

Figure 1.13 – Full Adder

A	B	Cin	Cout	S
0	0	0	0	0
0	0	1	0	1
0	1	0	0	1
0	1	1	1	0
1	0	0	0	1
1	0	1	1	0
1	1	0	1	0
1	1	1	1	1

For longer circuits, we can't able to draw full-adder as shown in the figure 1.13 on every usage, shortly the full adder can be

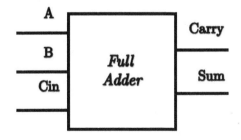

Figure: 1.15 – Simplified Representation of Full Adder

4-bit ripple carry adder:

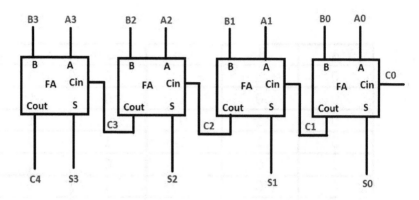

Figure 1.16 – 4 bit ripple carry adder

The above diagram illustrates the 4-bit ripple carry adder. As the name implies, two 4-bit binary numbers gets added with the help of the above circuit.

The inputs are of the form

A3	A2	A1	A0
+B3	B2	B1	B0
C S3	S2	S1	S0

The four bit adder leads to ripple carry delay. Here there will be a delay due to waiting operation. This delay operation was rectified by the Carry Look Ahead Adder (CLA). Similarly, the circuits for subtraction, multiplication and division will be designed using appropriate algorithms.

As the introductory perspective, it is enough to have same basic idea about ALU design.

CPU State Diagram:

Let us move on to the CPU state diagram. At any instant, the working CPU may be any of the following states,

(1)   Fetch State

(2)   Decode State

(3)   Execute State

Fetch State:

The fetch state will fetches the instruction from memory and make them ready for further processing. It is called as initial-active state.

Because the active CPU will undergo this state at initial time t.

Decode State:

The decode state will decodes the instruction then it will identify the relevant machine code. After that, it will move on to the execute state.

Execute State:

The execute state is responsible for the execution of the decoded instruction. After execution has over, it moves to initial-active state again.

CPU State Chart Diagram:

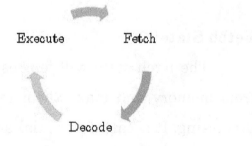

Execute   Fetch

Decode

Figure: 1.17 – State Chart Diagram for CPU

CHAPTER 01
INTRODUCTION TO PYTHON PROGRAMMING

" The man who graduates today and
Stops learning tomorrow is
Uneducated the day after! "

- Newton D. Baker

Python – is an effective programming language developed by "Guido van Rossum". Even though many programming languages are available, each has its own drawbacks. The evolution of new programming language will clears some drawback of the already existing programming language. But it may incur any other limitations in it. Before going through the concepts of Python, let us discuss few things about the programming languages.

We already know that, computer can understand only binary logic (0's and 1's) but it is very difficult to communicate with PC's via the binary language. Hence a translator like object is essential in order to translate the human language to binary language and vice versa.

A programming language can be defined as the syntax-oriented formally designed language which is used for the purpose of interacting with computers.

HARIPRASATH.P

1.1 Classification of Programming Languages:

The programming languages are broadly classified into 3 categories. They are, low level language, high level language and the middle level language. The low level language is one which provides no degree of abstraction and examples of it includes Assembly level language (Example : MOV A,B) which will instructs the computer to move content of B to A. As the consequence, the memory location A will have the value of B. The low level programming language may also include machine level language which is made by 0's and 1's. (Example: 01101010) which is absolutely not understandable by the human.

The middle level languages provides more degree of abstraction and effective user interactions with system but it is not so good when compared to the high level languages. Programming language C is a good example for the middle level language.

HARIPRASATH.P

The languages which are more effective and have very good interaction support are said to be high level languages. The high level languages should be converted into low level languages so that the machine can understand. Python is a good example for the high level language.

Some other examples for the high level language include Java, VB .NET, Perl.

Can you answer?

1. Classify: Programming languages.
2. Give examples for high level languages.
3. Why C is called as middle level language?
4. Which language is not understandable by the human? Give reason.
5. Write the necessity of Programming languages.

1.2 Python – Features:

As we discussed above, Python is the high level language which has various features as pointed below,

❶ The main feature is that it is a high level language; hence automatically the higher degree of abstraction is available.

② Python allow programmers to work with the variables in effective way which means that Python will support usage of variables with declaring them. In C, it is very essential to declare the variable at the beginning itself. In C++ we can declare variables anywhere in the program but before use. But in Python, we no need to bother about the variable declarations.

③ Python has various built-in data-structures. The data-structures include lists, dictionary, sets, tuples etc.

④ Python supports effective exception handling mechanisms. The exceptions can be handled effectively using exception handler functions.

⑤ The main feature is that, Python is available free of cost. (It is a freeware). The terminology freeware can be written as free+software. Without paying any money, we can easily download and use it.

HARIPRASATH.P

6 The syntax of Python language is very easy to learn and also to understand. No need for writing larger codes for performing simple tasks.

7 Python is an Object Oriented Programming (OOP) language, but it doesn't force to use class while you're programming. You can use it, if you are really interested.

8 We can say, the Python as the interpreted language which will execute the lines of code (programming statements) directly. Hence, it doesn't generate .obj file which means that no-compilation operation has been done.

9 The syntax of Python language is very similar to human language syntax. For example: printing hello uses the syntax *print ("Hello")*. That's all.. No need of having complex functions or codings.

HARIPRASATH.P

Can you answer?

1. List out any three features of Python.
2. Compare the variable declaration operation in C, C++ and Python.
3. Justify the Python Programming language is a free ware.
4. With suitable example, justify that Python has effective syntax.
5. What are the data-structures supported by Python as built-in?

1.3 The First Step:

In order to work with the Python, the first step is to start with IDLE. If you're ready with the Python IDLE. The prompt will wait for user input with the symbol ">>>" which makes you sure that you're reading for programming with Python.

The interpreter of the python can be quitted by pressing Ctrl + D. In order to stop the execution immediately, we have to press Ctrl + C.

The Python is an intention oriented language. The intention should be strictly followed in order to write a good programming.

The following points illustrate some measures that will make you to program well in Python.

1 Intention should be followed in an effective way.

2 The comment lines should be included for better understanding.

3 Variables should be written in a meaningful manner.

Consider the following example,

```
a=2;
if a==2:
print ("hi");
```

If you run the above code, it will show Syntax Error: expected an intended block which means that intention failure occurs. The Python language strictly follows intention. In order to make the above program in a correct way, we can modify it as follows,

```
a=2;
if a==2:
     print ("hi");
```

HARIPRASATH.P

Can you answer?

1. What happens if you press Ctrl + D and Ctrl + C if you are in Python IDLE?

2. Write few steps that have to be followed in order write effective code in Python.

3. With suitable example, prove Python is intention oriented language.

4. How to resolve the syntax error: "expected an intended block"?

5. Identify the error in the following code:

```
a=1;
b=2;
print ("b");
if(b==0):
print("Good Day");
```

1.4 Python – Print function:

The Print function is used to print the specified sentence or string that was quoted inside the function (or) we can say it prints the string which is passed as the parameter. The Print function uses the syntax, print("string name") or print('string name') or print("string name");

***Example* 1:**   print('a')

Output: a

The possible errors that you can do while working with the print function is the usage of **P**rint (capitalized P) in this case, the Python will produces Name Error which means it shows name 'Print' is not defined. If you miss the ' ' (quotes) it will produce the same name error.

Consider the following code to understand more about Print function in Python,

***Example* 2:**
```
print("Hari");
#Printing with double quotes
print('Deepika');
#Printing with single quote
print(type("Latha"));
#Refer type function
```
Output:
```
Hari
Deepika
<class 'str'>
```

Errorful Example:
```
Print("Hari");
```
#Usage of capitalized P that makes Name Error
```
print(Parandaman);
```
#Name Error due to missing of double quotes

Error Generated:

#Statement 1:

Traceback (most recent call last):
  File "C:\Python34\a1.py", line 1, in <module>
    Print("Hari");
NameError: name 'Print' is not defined

#Statement 2:

Traceback (most recent call last):
  File "C:\Python34\a1.py", line 1, in <module>
    print(Parandaman);
NameError: name 'Parandaman' is not defined

Can you answer?

1. What is Print function? Write its usage.
2. Write a Python code for printing the string "Welcome to PEC".
3. What are the possible errors that you may encounter while working with Print function? How to resolve it?
4. Is it works good? Print('Boolean Algebra')
5. Write the syntax of Print function. Give suitable example.
6. Define the Type Function and its usage.
7. How to print a string in Python?

1.4 Python – Comment Lines:

In the Python language, comment lines are classified into two different types. They are single line comments and multi line comments. The syntax for single line comment is #comment (The scope of the single line comment is only up to a line). During the execution, the comment lines are skipped. The Python multi-line comment has the syntax " " " .....n comment lines....." " "

Example 3: (Single line Comment)

```
print("Hari");
#Printing with double quotes
print('Deepika');
#Printing with single quote
print(type("Latha"));
#Refer type function
```

Description:

Here, S1, S2 and S3 which are started with # acts as a comment line and they will not be executed at any instance. It is used for user – understanding purpose only.

Example 4: **(Multi line Comment)**

```
print("Square root of a number");
"""
The above code will
prints the string
square root of a
number
"""
```

The comments are given only for the purpose of user understanding. The comment lines don't make any logical changes in the program since they are not allowed to execute at any case.

Can you answer?

1. What is the need of comment line?
2. List out different types of comment line.
3. What is single line comment? Give example.
4. Compare the differences between single and multi-line comments.
5. Is comments are essential? Justify.
6. Identify the output of the following code:

```
print("Good Evening")
#This statement will print the string Good
Evening
print("Happy Holidays")
"""
The second
print function
```

prints
Happy Holidays
"""

1.5 Variables:

Python has effective features for working with the variable. Generally, a variable is a memory location that was occupied in order to store the data. For example, in C language int a; is the variable declaration which occupies 2 bytes of memory for storing integer value and the memory location is addressed/named as a. As similar, working with Python variables has the following rules,

❶ The variable should start with [a-z/A-Z] or the underscore. Example: var, var_cart, _cartesian are the allowed type. ,score , +sen are not allowed.

❷ Variables are case sensitive which means that there is a difference between col and Col.

❸ Rather than starting, other parts of variable can be designed of [a-z/A-Z/letters/underscore]. Example: _coronary1

4 Variable should be meaningful one.

However the above rules are enough to design a variable in Python, to make sure of consistency, we have to use meaningful, shorter size and consistent variable names.

For example: If a variable is needed for storing an employee identification number, we have to follow the above rules, if so we get the variable name as *employee_identification_number* which is very long. Hence we have to optimizly change it as *e_id* which is understandable, small as well as meaningful.

1.5.1. Assigning Values to the variables:

The main need of variable is to reserve some sort of memory for storing some sort of information. To specify what information should be stored into a variable name, we have to use the assignment statement. The assignment of values to the variable involves single assignment as well as multiple assignments.

The single assignment will follow the syntax: *variable name = value.* The multiple assignment follow the syntax: *variable1 = variable2 = ... = variable n=value.*

***Example* 5: (Single Assignment)**
> K=24
> #Here, K is the variable

***Example* 6: (Multiple Assignment)**
> K = X = Y = 24
> #Here K, X and Y are the variables.

1.5.2. Printing the values of the variables using Print function:

We can print the value of the variable using the print function with the help of the following syntax: *print (variable name)* which means by passing variable name as a parameter to the built in print function we can get the value of the variable.

***Example* 7: (Printing value of the variable)**
> k=25
> print(k)

Output: 25

The possible error that you can make while working with variables include,

❶ Case Sensitivity Mistake – This mistake will leads to the name error which shows that the name is not defined.

❷ During printing contents of the variable, if you use quotes inside the print function print("K") let K be a variable, it just assume it as string and prints K instead of value of the variable K.

Errorful Example:

```
I=0
#The variable I is assigned with
value 0.
print(i)
#Case Sensitivity Mistake [Line 2]
t=3
#The variable t is assigned with 3.
print("t")
#Usage of double quotes consider t
as string
```

Output:

Line 1:

Traceback (most recent call last):

  File "<pyshell#7>", line 1, in <module>

    print(I)

NameError: name 'i' is not defined

Line 4:

Note that, in line 4, the desired output is value(t) ie, 3 but the output received is t which is due to the usage of double quote inside the print function.

Can you answer?

1. What is the need of variable?
2. How to print the values of the variable using print function?
3. State the rules for variable in Python.
4. Explain how to assign values to the variables.
5. What is multiple assignment? Give its syntax.
6. What are the possible mistakes that you can do while working with variables?
7. Identify the output of the following code:

```
t=1
x=2
t=t+1
print(t)
print("T")
print(x)
print(X)
```

8. Write a Python code for assigning values of the variable x,y,z as 2 and also print these values to the console also.
9. Write a Python code for implementation of single as well as multiple assignments.
10. Debug the errors in the following code:

```
T=t=5
```

print(t+T)

#This statement is written with intention of printing sum of t and T

print(X)

#This statement is written with intention of printing X on console.

1.6 Datatypes:

Python will support various data-types. The general built-in datatypes supported by Python includes numbers, string, list and tuples. Datatypes are one which defines the type of the data. We will discuss about numbers and strings in this section.

1.6.1. Numbers:

The Python numbers falls into various categories. It may of integer or float or double or even hexa-decimal also. Complex numbers are also supported by the Python. We can easily identify the data-type of variable using the type() function.

The type() function is used for identifying type of variable. The syntax is *type(variable name)*. During variable usage, we no need to specify the data-type of the variable because it was implicitly identified by the system software.

Consider the following example for learning the implicit type-conversion feature of the Python

Example 8: (Implicit Type Conversions)

```
T=5
#Implicitly the data-type is set
to integer.
T= "five"
#The type conversion made and it
changes data-type to string
T=4+5.5
#Changes the type of T to float
```

Now, the example 9 will illustrate about the number data-type which is supported by the Python language.

Example 9: (Number Datatype)

```
k=25
#Integer Number
k1=0.11
#Float Number
k2=0x11
#Hexa-decimal number which is
started with '0x'
k3=3+9j
#Complex Number
print(k)
```

```
print(k1)
print(k2)
print(k3)
```

Output:

25

0.11

17

(3+9j)

Note that type() function is used for identifying the type of a variable. The concept of type() function will discussed in upcoming chapters. Let us now understand how to work with the strings.

1.6.2 Strings:

Strings are the nothing but sequence of character. In Python strings are classified into three different categories. They are single quote string, double quote string and multi-quoted string.

A single quoted string is one in which the string is defined within a single quote, example: 'hello' similarly double quoted strings are of format "string" whereas the multi-quoted strings are of format ' ' 'string '''. The following example will illustrate such types of strings.

***Example* 10:**
(Strings)

```
X= "Cartesian  Product  of  the  given
equation";
    print(X)
    #Printing double quoted string
    Y= 'Cartesian  Product  of  the  given
equation';
    print(Y)
    #Printing single quoted string
    Z= ''' Cartesian
            Product
                Of the Given equation ''';
    print(Z)
    #Printing multi-quoted string
```

Output:

Cartesian Product of the given equation
Cartesian Product of the given equation
Cartesian
Product
of the given equation

Python supports various built-in functions for different string operations. Let we discuss some of the string functions here,

1.6.2.1. Capitalize function:

The main purpose of the capitalize function is to capitalize the first letter of the String that was specified. The syntax of the capitalize function is, *var_name.capitalize()*.

***Example* 11:**
(Capitalize Function)

X= "cartesian Product of the given equation";

print(X.capitalize())

output:

Cartesian Product of the given equation

In the above example, note that the character 'C' was capitalized.

1.6.2.2. Upper Case Conversion function:

It converts the whole string into the upper case format (Capitalize all). The syntax is of *string_holding_variable.upper()*.

***Example* 12:**
(Upper Function)

X= "cartesian Product of the given equation";

print(X.upper())

Output:

CARTESIAN PRODUCT OF THE GIVEN EQUATION

1.6.2.3. Boolean Functions:

The boolean functions comprises of isalpha, isdigit, isdecimal, isdigit, isidentifier, islower, isnumeric. The above functions will return only 2 values, one is true and another one is false value.

1 isdecmial() – is a boolean function that will check whether the variable holds decimal value / not. If it holds decimal value it returns true else it returns false.

2 isnumeric() – is a boolean function that will check whether the variable holds a numeric value/not. If it holds numeric value it returns true.

3 isalpha() – boolean function used for checking wheher the variable holds alpha-numeric value or not.

4 isdigit() – boolean valued function for checking digit/not.

5 Isidentifier() – boolean valued function for checking whether the variable holds identifier or not.

Example 13:
(Boolean Functions)

```
X="chemistry in action";
print(X.isdecimal())
print(X.isnumeric())
print(X.isalpha())
print(X.isdigit())
print(X.islower())
print(X.isidentifier())
```

Output:

```
False
False
False
False
True
False
```

As described above, the boolean functions return only *True / False* values. In addition to the above functions. There are many functions used for manipulating the string. One of the important functions is called as format() function which is discussed in the Section: 1.6.2.4.

Usage of built in functions makes task much easier and time – consuming one. Hence, for effective programming it is advisable to use such functions.

1.6.2.4. format() Method:

The format() method is used the formatting purpose of string. It will be effectively understandable by using the example given below

***Example* 14:**   **(format function)**
```
X= "India"
Y= "Country"
print("{0} is my {1}".format(X,Y));
```

Output:
India is my Country.

Can you answer?
1. What is implicit type conversion?
2. How type conversion performed in Python? Give suitable explanation.
3. List the number data-types supported by Python.
4. Write a Python code that adds two complex numbers.
5. Explain the different types of strings supported by Python.

6. Define Multi-quoted string.

7. Write a Python code for the implementation of different types of strings.

8. Give the syntax of Capitalize function.

9. List out some boolean functions and their uses.

10. Write Python code for implementation of any four boolean functions.

11. What is format() function? Give example.

1.7 Escape Sequences:

The escape sequences are one which are not printed in the console. They are just used for the purpose of alignment. As similar to C language, the escape sequence \n is used for making a text string to print in next line and \t is used for tab space.

***Example* 15:** **(Escape Sequences)**

X="Gandhiji \t - \t The Great National leader \n I love India!!!";

print(X)

Output:

Gandhiji   -   The Great National leader
I love India!!!

In the above example, you can easily identify the usage of escape sequence which puts a tab space and makes the string I love India to be printed on the separate line.

Case Study: license() Method:

The license method is used for the purpose of displaying history and license details of the Python. The syntax is: license().

Example **16:**
(License)
    license()
Output:
A. HISTORY OF THE SOFTWARE
==========================
Python was created in the early 1990s by Guido van Rossum at Stichting Mathematisch Centrum (CWI, see http://www.cwi.nl) in the Netherlands as a successor of a language called ABC. Guido remains Python's principal author, although it includes many contributions from others....

1.8. Keywords

Python has some reserved words called as keywords. The keywords are assigned with some pre-defined meaning. Hence, it should not be used as a variable name. The method help('keyword') returns the set of keywords that are supported by the Python.

```
and, as, assert, break, class,continue
 elif,else,except,def,del,for,finally
               from,
   global,if,import,in,is,not,or,pass
      return,try,while,with,yield.
```

***Example* 17:**   **(Keywords)**

    if a>2:

#usage of keyword if. The upcoming chapter describes this keyword.

    a=a+1

1.8.1. Error: Usage of Keyword as the variable name:

    Consider the following example, which tries to make the keyword as the variable name.

***Example* 18:**

(Error: Usage of Keyword as variable name)

    if=5;

    print(if);

Output:

    Invalid Syntax

Can you answer?

1. List any five keywords.

2. Give a Python code that illustrates the escape sequence.

3. How to get a history of Python? Is any special function available for it?

EXERCISE

Write the Python code for the following scenarios:

1 John wants to capitalize his string "cartesian product" at the whole

2 Mary would like to access the history of the Python using a single function.

3 Jim a small kid doesn't know whether the number is integer or numeric or alpha numeric or it falls on any other category. Write a Python code that helps Jim to identify the number "5.456" is of what type.

4 Latha wants to assign the value of variables *k*, *t* and *y* as 5 and for *x* as 3. And also she needs to perform type conversion on *k* in such a way that it value is as to be replaced by a string *calender*. Derive the Python code to do so.

5 Reason out the cause of the error in the following code:

```
assert=1
assert=assert+6;
print(assert);
```

6 Predict the output of the following Python code:

```
A=4
B=2
C=Y=Z=3
print(A)
print("{0}".format(C));
print(type(C));
D="Mica is an insulator";
print(D.capitalize());
print(D.isdecimal());
```

7 Predict the output of the following code:

```
A="Survey";
print(A);
print("A");
print('A');
print(A.upper());
A="45.4";
print(A);
print("a");
print('a');
```

8 Deepa wants to perform subtract the two complex numbers 2 + 4*j* and 4 + 9*j*. Write the Python code to perform so.

9 Is class is compulsory attribute in Python – Discuss.

****

*Note: For the solutions to the above exercise,
please visit www.hariprasath.org/python*

CHAPTER 02
BASIC CONCEPTS OF PYTHON PROGRAMMING

'' Learning is the eye of mind! ''

- A French Proverb

HARIPRASATH.P

In the previous chapter, we discussed about the introduction of Python language. In this chapter, we will continue with the basic concepts of the Python language. We are already familiar on working with Interactive Development Environment (IDLE). Let us start this chapter with knowing how to get user inputs.

2.1. Getting the input from the user:

In previous chapter, the inputs are directly specified in the program itself, but to give inputs in the run time, the Python language provides a function called as the *input()*. The syntax of this function is, *variable= input()*; Look at the following example,

***Example* 1**
[input() method]

```
print("Enter the value of A");
a= input();
print("You have entered"+a);
```

Input:
    Enter the value of A
    4

Output: You have entered 4.

The above program will illustrates the importance of the built-in function so called input().

***Example* 2**

#Getting and Displaying the age

```
print("Enter your age")
age=input();
print("Your age is"+age);
```

Input:

Enter your age

18

Output:

Your age is 18.

Case Study – Raw Strings:

Raw strings are special type of string with no special character which means if you declare the string as raw string, then it doesn't perform actual operation of the escal sequence rather it prints the escape sequence on the screen.

The syntax of the raw string is of print (*r* "String Sequence").

***Example* 3**

#Raw String Implementation

```
print (r "\n Hello \t Hey \t How are you?");
```

Output:

\n Hello \t Hey \t How are you?

Note:

In chapter 1, we discussed some of the escape sequences. In this chapter, we will discuss some other advanced escape sequences. In order to print the ' or " we have to use the escape sequence \ ' or \ ".

To print the single back slash, we have to use the syntax \ \ *String to be printed.*

***Example* 4**

#Escape Sequence Implementation

```
print("\\t");
print("\'Hi! Hello\'");
print("\a");
#Produces bell sound (beeps once)
```

Output:

```
\t
'Hi! Hello'
```

Can you answer?

1. What is Raw-string? Give example.
2. Get two numbers from the user and display on the console using Python.
3. How to create bell sound on screen? Give syntax.

2.2 Additional String Operations:

In the previous chapter, we have discussed some basic string operations. We will continue with some additional string operations in this chapter.

2.2.1. Lower Case Conversion:

The lower case conversion can be performed by using the syntax *var_name.lower()* which converts the string into lower case. Consider the following example,

Example 5   **#Lower Case Conversion**
    T= "COMPUTER"
    print(T.lower());
Output:
    computer

2.2.2. Title Case Conversion:

The title case conversion will makes the first letter as capitalized at each word.

Example 6   **#Title Case Conversion**
    T= "COSMIC RAYS"
    print(T.title());
Output:
    Cosmic Rays

2.2.3. String Replacement:

We can easily replace the string with the help of this built-in function. The string replacement follows the synta *var_name.replace("Existing String", "Replaceable*

String"); Let us go through the example given below

Example 7

#String Replacement

    T= "COMPUTER"

    print(T.replace("PU", "GO"));

Output:

    COMGOTER

2.2.4. Swap Case Conversion:

    Swap case conversion will make the first letter of the string to be displayed small and all other characters are displayed as capitalized.

Example 8

#Swap Case Replacement

    T= "Palindrome"

    print(T.swapcase())

Output:

    pALINDROME

2.2.5. Translate Method:

    translate() method is used for simple encoding operation in which it uses a table which it has some set of strings and their equivalent translation words. Such table is called as translate table and it can be created by the syntax, tab_name=maketrans(actual_value, value_to_be_encoded). After that, usage of syntax variable_name.translate(tab_name) will make you to perform translation.

Example 9

#Translate Method

```
#Translation Table Creation
X= "ABC"
Y= "123"
Z=maketrans(X,Y);
```

```
#Translation Operation
q= "A for Apple, B for Ball, C for Cat";
print(q.translate(Z));
```

Output:

1 for 1pple , 2 for 21ll, 3 for 31t

In version Python3, the translate method is of

Example 10

#Translate Method for Python Version 3

```
a1 = 'chemis'
a2 = '123456'
s = 'Chemistry in action!!!'
print(s.translate({ord(x): y for (x, y) in zip(a1, a3)}))
```

Output:

C23456try 5n a1t5on!!!

Can you answer?

1. Explain title case conversion.

2. Write a Python code for encoding "abcdefg" as "1234567" in the string "The Digestive System Concepts(Human Physiology)"

3. Perform the following change cases on the string "Mr.Nethaji is my botany staff":

(a) Swap case   (b) Title Case   (c) Lower Case

4. Replace the string raser with the word 'lephant' in the word "Eraser" .

2.3. len function:

The purpose of the len function is used for identifying the length of the string. Consider the string "pendrive" which is stored in variable x, then the function called len(x) will return the length as 8.

The syntax of the len function is *len(object)*. The following example illustrates the len function

Example 11   **(Len function)**

```
X= "car"
print(len(X))          #Returns       the
value 3 [C A R] → [1 2 3]
```

Output:

3

Consider that if my string has a blank space. On such cases, how my len function works. Len method takes blank spaces also for consideration. The following example illustrates this concept,

Example 12
(Len Function – Miscellaneous Case)
        Y= "one space"
        print(len(Y));
Output:
        9

Can you answer?
1. How will you calculate the length of the string in Python?
2. What will be the output of len() function in the following cases?
        (a) "EXPLAIN"
        (b) "Suffering from"
        (c) "tentative examination 2014"
3. Predict the output of the following code:
        y= "binomial theorem";
        print(len(Y));
4. State the reason for the output of len("New Year"); is 8.

2.4 Type Function:

The type function is used for identification of the data-type in most cases. The type function helps us to implicit type conversion of Python language. The type function will gives the type of the variable.

It is not a difficult task to work with such function. It is very easy to identify the type of any variable using a function. Not only the variable, we can also pass the immediate input (say type(3)) to identify its type.

The syntax of the type function is of *type*(object_name) or *type*(variable_name) which will return the datatype of the object or the variable. The following example will illustrates the type function,

***Example* 13**   **(Type Function)**

```
X=4
print(type(X))
print(type(5))
```

Output:

```
<class 'int'>
<class 'int'>
```

The reason for the above shown output <class 'int'> defines the variable holding value (X=4) is of type integer which means 4 is integer and the second output states that 5 is also an integer value.

The output of the type function may be of any one of the following, <class 'float'> which states the passed parameter is of type float, <class 'str'> which means that the passed parameter is of type string, <class 'complex'> which means that the passed parameter is of type complex number. The following example will help you to understand more about type function.

Example 14   **(Type Function)**

```
X=3
Y=4.22
Z=3+4j
M= "member"
print(type(X))
print(type(Y))
print(type(Z))
print(type(M))
```

Output:

```
<class 'int'>
<class 'float'>
<class 'complex'>
<class 'str'>
```

Thus, the type function is used for the purpose of identifying the type of an object which is passed as a parameter to it.

2.4.1. Implicit Type Conversion:

The Python programming will support the implicit type conversion which can be easily understandable by the type() function. Let us consider a variable X holds the value 4 (which integer) initially, after that if the variable is assigned with the value 6.2, the Python interpreter changes the type(X) to 6.2 implicitly which is explained in the example given below, (Example 15)

Example **15**
(Type Function)

```
X=4
print(type(X))
X=6.2
print(type(X))
```

Output:

```
<class 'int'>
<class 'float'>
```

2.4.2. All the contents that are within quotes are considered as strings!

In the Python language, the contents inside the quotes are considered as the strings. It will be explained by the following example,

Example **16**   **(Type Function)**

```
X= "2.455"
print(type(X))
```

Output:

```
<class 'str'>
```

In the above example, the type function should return the type as float, since the the value of X is 2.455, but it is specified within quotes hence the Python will consider it as the type string. Hence, we can justify that, all quoted contents are assumed as string in Python.

Can you answer?

1. How to identify the type of an object in Python?

2. Predict the output of the following code:

    type(2.45)
    type(356.67543)
    type("Hello World")
    type("3+2j")
    type(2+6j)
    type("2.22")
    type(5.356)

3. Explain the implicit type conversion with respect to the type function.

4. Is all the contents that are specified inside double quotes are considered as strings? Justify your answer.

2.5. Operators and Expressions:

The Operators are one which is used for performing the operations with the operands. Python supports various different operators for performing different operations which are stated below,

2.5.1. Arithmetic Operators:

Addition Operator (+)is used for performing the addition activity which follows the syntax Operand 1 + Operand 2 which produces the output as the sum of Operand 1 and Operand 2. Similarly for subtraction (-) operator is used, multiplication uses (*) operator and division uses (/) operator. The floor function can be established using the operator (//). The modulus operation can be performed with (%) operator. To specify, power (Eg: 2^n) python has ** operator (Eg: 2 ** n)

Example 17

(Arithmetic Operators)

```
X=5
Y=4
Z=X+Y
# Addition Operation
print(Z)
Z=X-Y
# Subtraction Operation
print(Z)
Z=X*Y
# Multiplication Operation
print(Z)
Z=X/Y
# Division Operation
print(Z)
Z=X%Y
```

```
# Modulo Operation
print(Z)
Z=X//Y
# Floor Operation
print(Z)
Z=X**Y
# Power Operation
print(Z)
```

Output:
```
9
1
20
1.25
1
1
625
```

2.5.2 Shifting Operators:

The left shift operation can be performed by the << operator and similarly the right shift can be performed by >> operator.

***Example* 18**
(Shifting Operators)
```
X=5
Y=24
print(X>>Y)
#Right Shifting Operation
print(Y<<X)
```

#Left Shifting Operation

Output:
    0
    768

2.5.3 Bitwise Operators:

The bitwise operators include bitwise OR, bitwise AND, bitwise XOR, bitwise invert operators which is explained in the following example.

Example **19**

(Bitwise Operators)

```
X=5
Y=2
print(X&Y)
#Bitwise AND Operation
print(X|Y)        #Bitwise OR Operation
print(X^Y)        #Bitwise XOR Operation
print(~Y)         #Invert Operation
```

Output:
    0
    7
    7
    -3

Let we discuss how the output arrives. Here X is initialized with 5 and Y is initialized with 2. Now consider X&Y (bitwise AND

Operation) the binary representation of 5 is 0101 and for 2 it is 0010. The bitwise AND will gives 0000 which is 0.

Similarly, for the second output the binary values get OR'ed which gives 0111 which is 7 base-10 representation. For the last output, the value of Y is inverted hence it produces the output -3.

***Example* 20**

(Printing same string multiple times)

    X= 'car'
    Y= X*5
    print(Y)

Output:

    carcarcarcarcar

Such kinds of operations (shown in Example 20) are made very simple and it adds more advantage to the Python Programming.

2.5.4. Boolean Operators

The Boolean operators are one which returns only two values. They are *True* and *False*. Logically we can say [0,1]. The following example will explain the concept of Boolean operators.

Boolean operators includes <(less than) operator, > (greater than) operator, less than or equal to operator (<=) , greater than or equal to operator (>=), equal to operator (==), not equal to operator (!=)

***Example* 21**

(Boolean Operators)

```
X= 2
Y= 5
print(X>Y)
#Greater than Operator
print(X<Y)
#Less than Operator
print(X<=Y)
#Less than or equal to Operator
print(X>=Y)
#Greater than or equal to Operator
print(X==Y)
#equal to operator
print(X!=Y)
#Not equal to operator
```

Output:

```
False
True
True
False
False
True
```

2.5.5. Expressions:

The expressions are formed by the combination of operators and operands. In Python the evaluation of the expression will follow certain order of evaluation which will be discussed in the next section. In this section, let us discuss about simple expressions. Consider the expression $x = y + z$, which will adds y and z and stores the result to x. The following example illustrates how to work with simple expressions.

***Example* 22**   **(Expressions)**

```
X= 2
Y=5
Z=X+Y
```
Simple Expression.

Output:

        7   -3

Can you answer?

1. Design a simple calculator that takes inputs from user and produces the user specified operation.

2. Explain the Boolean operators in Python with examples.

3. Print a string 'colonel west', 25 times by writing a single line of code in Python.

2.6. Order of Evaluation:

The order of evaluation defines the certain order that the Python follows in order to execute the expressions.

The order of evaluation can be expressed by the BEMDAS rule.

2.6.1 BEMDAS rule:

The BEMDAS rule states the order as

Brackets →

Exponents →

Division →

Addition →

Subtraction

as the order of evaluating expression ie, whenever an expression has more than one operator in such case it will follow the BEMDAS rule. It evaluates the contents inside the bracket first, then the priority goes to exponents, followed by division, addition operations and finally the subtraction will be performed.

***Example* 23   (Order of Evaluation)**

```
print(2+3* - 4+3)
```

Output:

- 7

***Example* 24   (Order of Evaluation)**

```
x=(2+3)*(2-3)+(2/4)
y=(5/2)+(8*(5-4)+(4/3))
z=(9+5-(2+9)+4*(4/2))
k=x*(x+1)-y*(y-1)+z*(z-1)
print(x,"\n",y,"\n",z,"\n",k)
```

Output:

-4.5

11.833333333333334

11.0

-2.444444444444457

Now let us discuss how to write the general mathematical equation into Python executable format. Consider the expression $\left(\frac{x}{y}\right)+\left(\frac{y}{z}\right)-\left(\frac{x+y}{x-y}\right)$. Let we know how to express in the program.

For $\left(\frac{x}{y}\right)$ it should be expressed as (x/y) and similarly the second part of expression is expressed as (y/z) and the third part of expression is expressed as $(x+y)/(x-y)$ and finally, the whole expression is expressed as $(x/y) + (y/z) - ((x+y)/(x-y))$ so that the Python can understand it.

Example **25**

(Order of Evaluation)

$(a+b)^2 = a^2 + b^2 + 2ab$

```
print ("Enter A")
a=int(input())
print ("Enter B")
b=int(input())
c=(a+b)*(a+b)
```

```
d=(a*a)+(b*b)+(2*a*b)
print("L.H.S",+c)
print("R.H.S",+d)
```

Output:

```
Enter A
5
Enter B
4
L.H.S
81
R.H.S
81
```

Can you answer?

1. How to express the followings in Python code?

(a) $\dfrac{1}{\sqrt{a^2+b^2}}$ (b) $\dfrac{-b\pm\sqrt{b^2-4ac}}{2a}$ (c)

$\dfrac{n!}{r!(n-r)!}$ (d) $e^{i\theta}$

(e) $\dfrac{1}{\sqrt{ax+bx}}$ (f) $(x+y)(x^3+y^3-2xy)$ (g)

$2x+y\Big/x(x-y^4)$

2. State BEMDAS rule.

3. Predict the output of the following code:

```
x=(2+3)*(2-3)+(2/4)
y=(5/2)+(8*(5-4)+(4/3))
z=(9+5-(2+9)+4*(4/2))
```

```
k=x*(x+1)-y*(y-1)+z*(z-1)
print(k)
```

4. Write a Python code to find

(a) Square and Cube of the given number.

(b) To check whether $(a+b)^3$ is equivalent to (a^2+b^2+2ab)

(c) To find the value of the expression $\left(\dfrac{x}{y}\right)+\left(\dfrac{y}{z}\right)-\left(\dfrac{x+y}{x-y}\right)$ where x, y and z values should be obtained from the user at the run-time.

Note: For the solutions to the above exercise, please visit *www.hariprasath.org/python*

HARIPRASATH.P

CHAPTER 03
CONTROL FLOW STATEMENTS IN PYTHON

" Tell Me! And I Forget!
Teach Me! And I may Remember!
Involve Me! And I Learn! "
                    - Benjamin Franklin

In the previous chapter, we discussed about the basic concepts of Python language. In this chapter, we will discuss about the control flow statements that are available in the Python language. In Python, the control flow statements includes if statement, if – else statement, if – elif – else statement and some looping statements.

3.1. If statement:

The main purpose of the if statement is to check the truthfulness of the condition. If the condition gets true then the statements inside the if block will gets executed or else the control skips the if block and the else statement will gets executed. The syntax for if-statement is

```
if(condition):
        #Statements for the if-block
```

***Example* 1**   **(Simple If – statement)**
```
x=5
if(x==5):
        print("The value of X is 5");
print("Program Ends...");
```
Output:
```
The value of X is 5
Program Ends...
```

In the above example, we can identify the logic of if statement. Initially, the value of x is initialized to 5 and the if condition checks whether x is equal to 5 or not. If x value is satisfied with the checking constraint (ie, 5) then the control reaches inside the if block and the code inside the if block will gets executed (i.e, in our example, the code inside the if block is a print function). Thus the print function will be executed on the console.

Let us consider a if – statement with else condition which is shown in the example 3.2, In the example 3.1, if the condition is not satisfied, the if block was just skipped whereas in case of if – else statement, if condition not satisfied, then else block will be executed. The syntax of if-else statement is,

if(condition):
        #Statements for if – block
    else:
    #Statements for else – condition

***Example* 2**   **(If – Else Statement)**
    X = 6
    Y = 4
    if(X==Y):
            print("Both X and Y are equal")
    else:
            print("X and Y are not equal")

In the above example, the condition X==Y fails because (6!=4) hence the else part gets executed and prints the result as "X and Y are not equal".

The final type of if-condition is of if-elif-else statement in which initially it will check for condtion *X==Y?* if fails then flow goes for checking another condition (let it be *X==Z?*) similarly it will check certain *n* sorts of conditions for true/false. If any one gives true value, then the code inside that condition will be executed. If all of the condition, produces the false value then at such cases it just executes the code inside the else statement. The syntax of if-elif-else statement is shown below:

```
if(condition1):
        #Statement 1
elif(Condition 2):
        #Statement 2
else
        #Statement 3
```

Example 3

(If – Elif – Else Statement)

```
X = 6
Y = 4
if(X==Y):
        print("X is equal to Y");
elif(X>Y):
        print("X is greater than Y");
```

```
        elif(X<Y):
                print("X is less than Y");
        else:
                print("Oop! Unpredictable");
```
Output: X is greater than Y.

The above example shows the finding greatest of two numbers using a simple if-elif-else statement. Now, let we discuss some programs based on the if-conditions.

Example 4
#Odd or even
```
        t=int(input("Enter a number"))
        if(t%2==0):
                print("The number is even");
        else:
                print("The number is odd");
```
Output:
```
        Enter a number
        5
        The number is odd
```

Example 5
#Identifying Eligible to Vote / Not
```
        age=int(input("Enter your age"))
        if(age>=18):
                print("Eligible");
        else:
                print("Not Eligible ");
```

```
        age=18-age;
        print("You        have        to        wait
until",+age,"years");
```

Output:
```
    Enter your age
    5
    Not eligible
    You have to wait until 13 years
```


Example 6
#Simple Login Form
```
    print("SIGN UP!");
    user_name=input("Enter uname");
    password=input("Enter pwd");
    cpass=input("Enter pwd again");
    if(password==cpass):
        print("Success!");
        u_na=input("Enter uname");
        if(u_na==user_name):
            pw=input("Enter pwd");
            if(pw==password):
                print("Success!");
        else:
        print("Error!");
        else:
        print("Check the Username");
    else:
```

print("Error in Password");

Output:
SIGN UP!
Enter the user name
HARI
Enter the password
PRIYA
Enter the password again
PRIYA
Success! Login Now!...
Enter the user name
HARI
Enter the password
PRIYA
Success! Logged In! Welcome!

The above example illustrates the effectiveness of Python. In C, the string compare operation is very difficult. To do so, we have to implement string.h header file followed by we have to use strcmp() function. Such kinds of drawbacks are avoided in Python language.

Example 7
#Simple Calculator

```
v1=int(input("Enter the First Operand"))
v2=int(input("Enter the Second Operand"))
print("1 - Addition \n 2 - Subtraction \n 3 -
Multiplication \n 4 - Division \n")
v3=int(input("Enter the Operator"))
```

```python
        if(v3==1):
                print(v1+v2)
        elif(v3==2):
                print(v1-v2)
        elif(v3==3):
                print(v1*v2)
        elif(v4==4):
                print(v1/v2)
        else:
                print("Check your Input! Operator Incorrect!");
```

Output:

Enter the First Operand   4
Enter the Second Operand   3
 1 - Addition
 2 - Subtraction
 3 - Multiplication
 4 - Division
Enter the Operator   1
        7

Can you answer?

1. What are control flow statements?
2. Give the syntax of if-elif-else statement.
3. Design a simple calculator that performs modulo, left shift and right shift.
4. Write a code to find whether the given number is a positive number or not.
5. Derive the Python code for simple login form.

HARIPRASATH.P

6. Write the differences between if, if-else and if-elif-else statements.

7. How string comparison varies in C and Python?

8. Write a Python program for checking whether the given character is a vowel or not.

3.2 While Loop

The while loop will gets executed if and only if the condition becomes true which means before entering the looping statement it will check whether the condition has been satisfied or not. If the condition yields true value (ie, satisfied) in such cases it will execute the while loop continuously until the condition becomes false. If condition gets failed then the loop gets terminated / skipped. The syntax of the while loop is given by,

```
while condition :
        Looping statements
```

Example 8
#Simple While loop
[For True Condition]
```
A=5
while A==5:
        print ("Value of A is 5");
        A=A-1;
```
Output: Value of A is 5

Example 9
#Simple While loop
[For False Condition]

```
A=2
while A==5:
        print ("Value of A is 5");
print("OOP! Loop gets terminated!");
```

Output:

OOP! Loop gets terminated!

The above two examples illustrates the true and false condition of the while loop. Let us discuss more about while loop in upcoming examples.

Example 10
#Armstrong number/not

```
n = int(input("Enter a number: "))
sum = 0
temp = n
while temp > 0:
        mo = temp % 10
        sum += mo ** 3
        temp //= 10

if n == sum:
        print("The    Input    Number    is
Armstrong!")
    else:
        print("Sorry! Its not Armstrong!")
```

Output:
>   Enter a number: 4
>   Sorry! Its not Armstrong!

Can you answer?
1. Write the syntax of while loop.
2. Write a Python code for finding the string entered is palindrome or not using string functions.
3. Implement a simple while loop in Python for checking whether the sum of digits of a number is 9 or not.

3.3 For Loop

In Python, the for loop uses the range function. The loop will gets iterated with the help of range function. The syntax of for loop is of

>   *for var_name in range(initial, final):*
>   *Looping statements*

Example 11
#Simple for loop
>   for i in range(1,2):
>   print("Hello");

Output: Hello

The logic behind the code in Example 11 is that, *the for – in loop gets executed in the following logic*

>   *for(i=1; i<2; i++) then execute the loop.* At first step, i is initialized to the value 1, now the

condition 1<2 satisfied and the loop gets executed that is, 'hello' will gets printed on console. In next case, i becomes 2, here 2<2 condition gets false and loop gets terminated! Let we discuss more about the for-loop in the following examples.

Example 12
#Factorial of a number

```
get = int(input("Enter a number: "))
f = 1
if get < 0:
        print("Check the input!");
else:
        for i in range(1,get + 1):
                f = f*i
print("The factorial of",get,"is",f)
```

Output:

```
Enter a number: 4
The factorial of 4 is 24
```

Example 13
#Displaying Prime Number in a range

```
begin = int(input("
        Beginning range: "))
end = int(input("End range: "))
for i in range(begin,end + 1):
        if i > 1:
```

```
            for t in range(2,i):
                    if (i % t) == 0:
                    break
            else:
                    print(i)
```

Output:
Beginning range: 10
End range: 50
11
13
17
19
23
29
31
37
41
43
47

Can you answer?
1. What is range function? Give its syntax.
2. Write a Python code for finding sum of N natural numbers.
3. Illustrate a Python code for matrix addition of 2x2 matrix.
4. Write Python code for multiplication tabulation.

5. Write a Python code for Pascal triangle implementation.
6. Explain how it works?
   for i in range(1,4):

3.4 Break Statement:

The purpose of the break statement is to halt the execution. The syntax of the break statement is very simple. It uses a simple keyword called as 'break'.

For example, refer the example noticed by the number 13.

3.5 Continue Statement:

The main purpose of continue statement is to skip the other parts of the loop and starts executing the next iteration of the loop in an effective way. It uses a keyword called continue.

Example 14
#Continue Statement
```
A=1
while A<=10:
A=A+1;
 if(A==5):
        continue;
print ("Hello");
```

Output:
Hello

Can you answer?
1. Differentiate between break and continue statement.
2. Write a Python code with the implementation of break and continue statement.
3. What will be the output of the Python code given below:

```
A=1
while A<=3:
    A=A-1;
    if(A==1):
        continue;
    print ("Hello");
```

4. Write the Python code for finding cube root and square root of the user given input number.
5. Establish the simplicity of Python in Control flow statements.
6. Identify the errors in the following source code and rewrite it:

```
Begin=Input();
End=Input();
for i in range(begin,end + 1):
        if i > 1
            for loop t in range(2,i):
                if (i % t) == 0:
                brake
```

HARIPRASATH.P

elif:

        printf(i)

7. Write a Python for the finding perfect number or not.

8. Differentiate between

    (a) While loop

    (b) For loop of Python.

9. When to use continue? Discuss.

3.6 FUNCTIONS

We already know that, there are two different types of functions available. They are (1) Built In (or) Pre – defined functions and the second one is (2) User Defined Functions. This chapter will discuss about the user defined functions. Let us know how to create a function.

3.6.1. User Defined Functions:

The user defined functions are one which are created by the user. We can easily create and work with functions. Creation of functions increases the modularity concept. The function creation is very simple in python. The syntax for creating user defined function is of

def *function_name*(parameters):

        #Code inside the function

Let we understand more about the function creation in the following examples.

Example 15
#*Function creation*

```
def abc():
```
#Function name is abc and no arguments passed

```
        print("Hello");
```

Output:

Nothing will be displayed.

In the example 15, the output doesn't produce because we just created the function but we didn't call it. The function will gets executed whenever it has been called. The syntax for calling the function is very simple, it is *function _ name (arguments)*. Let us alter the above code.

Example 16
#*Calling a function*

```
def abc():
```
#Function name is abc and no arguments passed

```
        print("Hello");
        abc()
```

Output:

Hello

In the above code, the function gets called by the statement abc() and the code inside the function is executed. As a result, hello is printed on console as the output.

Example 17

#Function with a single parameter

```
def f1(a):
        a=a+1;
        print(a)
        a=a-1;
        print(a)
        a=a*1;
        print(a)
        print("End of Function f1");
def f2(b):
        b=b+2;
        print(b)
        b=b-2;
        print(b)
        b=b*2;
        print(b)
f1(5)
f2(10)
```

Output:

```
6
5
5
End of Function f1
12
10
20
```

In the above code, two functions f1 and f2 are created and called. The values to the function are passed during the calling operation. Let us know how to pass value of the function at runtime in the example 18 given below.

Example 18

#Function with single parameter passing value at runtime

```
def f1(a):
        a=a+1;
        print(a)
         a=a-1;
        print(a)
        a=a*1;
        print(a)
        print("End of Function f1");
def f2(b):
        b=b+2;
        print(b)
        b=b-2;
        print(b)
        b=b*2;
         print(b)
x=int(input("Enter value for Function 1"))
f1(x)
y=int(input("Enter value for Function 2"))
f2(y)
```

Output:

Enter value for Function 1   :   4

5

4

4
End of Function f1
Enter value for Function 2   :   5
7
5
10

3.6.2. Function with multiple parameters:

In the previous examples, we have discussed about the functions with a single parameter. Now let us discuss a function with multiple parameters.

Example 19

#Function with multiple parameter passing value at runtime

 # A Simple Calculator Implemented using Function

 # Function with two parameters.

```
def add(a,b):
    c=a+b;
    print("Addition Result",c)
def sub(a,b):
    c=a-b;
    print("Subtraction Result",c)
def mul(a,b):
    c=a*b;
    print("Multiplication Result",c)
print("Enter your choice \n 1.Addition \n
2.Subtraction \n 3. Multiplication \n");
```

```python
ch=int(input());
if(ch==1):
    a=int(input("Enter A value"));
    b=int(input("Enter B value"));
    add(a,b)
elif(ch==2):
    a=int(input("Enter A value"));
    b=int(input("Enter B value"));
    sub(a,b)
elif(ch==3):
    a=int(input("Enter A value"));
    b=int(input("Enter B value"));
    mul(a,b)
else:
    print("Invalid Choice");
```

Output:

Enter your choice
 1.Addition
 2.Subtraction
 3. Multiplication
1
Enter A value   5
Enter B value   3
Addition Result   8

3.6.3. Local Variables

The local variables are one which is declared inside the function. In the coding

(Example 19), *c* is a local variable which gets used and declared inside the function.

3.6.4. Default Argument Value:

We can able to pass the value for the argument in the function definition itself, if it is so then it is said to be default argument value. It uses the following syntax *def function _ name (parameter _name = value, …).*

The following example will illustrate how to pass the value as default argument value.

Example 20

#Function with multiple parameter passing value at runtime

 # A Simple Calculator Implemented using Function with default argument value

 # Function with two parameters.

```
def add(a,b=3):
        c=a+b;
        print("Addition Result",c)
def sub(a,b=4):
        c=a-b;
        print("Subtraction Result",c)
def mul(a,b=5):
        c=a*b;
        print("Multiplication Result",c)
print("Enter your choice \n 1.Addition \n
2.Subtraction \n 3. Multiplication \n");
```

```
ch=int(input());
if(ch==1):
        a=int(input("Enter A value"));
        add(a)
elif(ch==2):
        a=int(input("Enter A value"));
        sub(a)
elif(ch==3):
        a=int(input("Enter A value"));
        mul(a)
else:
print("Invalid Choice");
```

Output:

Enter your choice

1.Addition

2.Subtraction

3. Multiplication

1

Enter A value   3

Addition Result   6

In the above example, the value of A is obtained from the user during the run-time whereas B is initiated with default argument value using the '=' operator. Hence while running, A value is obtained from user and B value is taken directly and produces the result.

3.6.5 Keyword Arguments

The Keyword arguments are used whenever if we have many parameters and need to pass value for some of them alone. The keyword arguments are explained in the example 21.

Example 21

```
#Keyword Arguments
def Key(a,b,c=8):
        t=b*b;
        x=t-(4*a*c);
        print("The value of x is",x);
print("Evaluation of b2-4ac");
print("Enter the A value \n");
f1=int(input());
print("Enter the B value \n");
f2=int(input());
Key(a=f1,b=f2)
#Here value passed to a and b alone.
```

Output:

Evaluation of b2-4ac

Enter the A value

5

Enter the B value

4

The value of x is -144

Example 22   *#Keyword Arguments*

```
def k(c,a=1,b=2):
        print(a+b+c);
k(4)
```

Output: 7

3.6.6. The Return statement

The function may return a value and it may be stored inside a variable. For such operations, the return keyword is used. The return statement should be used inside the function return(v_name); is the syntax for return statement.

Example 23

     #Return Statement

```
def k(c,a=1,b=2):
        return(a+b+c);
x=k(4)
print(x);
```

Output:

     7

In the above example, the function 'k' returns the sum of a,b,c and the return statement will transfer the control to the calling statement and hence the assignment *x=k(4)* makes the return value of the function to be assigned to the variable *k*. Hence *x* holds (a+b+c) respectively.

3.6.7. The Pass Statement:
If we want to create an empty function, in such cases we have to use the pass statement. The syntax is the usage of pass keyword.

Example 24   ***#Pass Statement***

```
def pas():
        pass            #Empty Function
    pas()
```

Output:
None

Can you answer?

1. What is a function? Give its type.
2. Implement a simple calculator that performs modulo division, left and right shift operations using a function.
3. Write a Python code for finding the correctness of $(a+b)^2 = a^2 + b^2 + 2ab$ using function. Use the concept of Keyword Argument and calculate the LHS and RHS using different functions.
4. Write a Python code for implementation of return and pass statements.
5. Establish a Python code for the implementation of Fibonacci series using function (use recursive function concept)
6. Write a Python code for the implementation of the matrix calculator using function which will perform matrix addition, multiplication and

transpose of matrix. (Implement the operations in separate functions)

7. What are pre-defined functions? Explain the followings:
   (a) range()
   (b) len()
   (c) type()

8. Write the Python code for implementation of following statements
   (a) break
   (b) pass
   (c) return

9. How functions are useful? Discuss with example.

CHAPTER 04
DATA STRUCTURES OF PYTHON

'' Those are fools however learned
Who have not learned to walk
With the world ''

- Thiruvalluvar

Python provides various built-in data structures. They are listed as followed,

1. List
2. Tuples
3. Dictionary
4. Sets

Let we discuss briefly about each of the above in detail.

4.1. List

List is nothing but a collection of items in sequence way. It is similar as array. We can store data's in a sequential way and hence the operations are made easy. For such sequential storage process, the Python provides an effective data-structure so called as lists. We can create the list with the following syntax,

List_Name = ['item 1', 'item 2'..............'item n']

Example 1
#Creation of list

```
list1=['a','b','c','d','e','f','g','h'];
print("List1 created!");
```
Output: List1 Created

The above shown example will just create a list. Let us see how to print the elements of list using the for loop.

Example 2
#Printing the elements of list
```
list1=['a','b','c','d','e','f','g','h'];

print(list1);

#simple printing using print() method

for item in list1:

    print(item);

#printing list item in for loop
```

Output:
```
['a', 'b', 'c', 'd', 'e', 'f', 'g', 'h']
a
b
c
d
e
f
g
h
```

4.2. Operations on List:
4.2.1. Finding the length of the list:

In order to find the length of the list we can use the method called len(). The syntax is len(list_name).

Example 2
#Printing the elements of list

        list1=['a','b','c','d','e','f','g','h'];
        print(len(list1));

Output: 8

                Length(List1)=8

4.2.2. Adding contents to the list:

If we want to add contents into the list, we can use the syntax as follows

    List_name.append('content_to_be_added');

The above syntax will add the content to the last end of the list. The example 3 will illustrates how to add contents to the list.

Example 3
#Printing the elements of list

        list1=['a','b','c','d','e','f','g','h'];
        print("Before Appending",list1);
        list1.append('k');
        print("After Appending",list1);

Output

Before Appending ['a', 'b', 'c', 'd', 'e', 'f', 'g', 'h']

After Appending ['a', 'b', 'c', 'd', 'e', 'f', 'g', 'h', 'k']

4.2.3. Sorting the list

The list can be sorted in ascending order using the syntax list_name.sort() which makes the list to be sorted.

Example 4
#Sorting the elements of list

```
l1=['car','van','auto' ,'bus'];
l1.sort()
print(l1)
l2=['4','6','7','1','3','2'];
l2.sort()
print(l2)
```

Output:

```
['auto', 'bus', 'car', 'van']
['1', '2', '3', '4', '6', '7']
```

In the above example, list 1 and 2 are sorted whereas l1 is sorted alphabetically and l2 is sorted numerically in ascending order.

4.2.4. Deleting items from the list:

We can delete the items from the list using the syntax del list_name[item_number]. Consider a list as shown below

If I would like to delete book from the list, we can use the syntax as listname (say l1), then del l1[3] where 3 is the location of the book in the list. Hence it will be deleted from the list.

Example 5
#Deleting the elements of list
```
l1=['pen','pencil','eraser','book','scale','note'];
del l1[3];
print(l1)
```
Output:
```
['pen', 'pencil', 'eraser', 'scale', 'note']
```

4.2.5. Count Method:

There may be a possibility of having duplicate records in the list. In order to count the duplicate records that are available in the list, we have to use the count method. The syntax is list_name.count('item');

Example 6
#Count Method Implementation
```
ab=['cat','rat','cat','cat','fox','lion','cat'];
t=ab.count('cat');
l=ab.count('lion');
print ("Total No of cat in the list",t)
print ("Total No of lion in the list",l)
```
Output:
```
Total No of cat in the list 4
Total No of lion in the list 1
```

4.2.6. Insert Method

In the append operation we can able to add the items into the end of the list. If we want to add the item at the specific index, then such cases, we have to go for the insert method. The insert method will add the item into the desired location.

The syntax of insert method is list.insert(index,'item');

Example 7

#Insert Method Implementation

```
ab=['cat','rat','cat','cat','fox','lion','cat'];
ab.insert(0,'Tiger');
print(ab)
```

Output:

['Tiger', 'cat', 'rat', 'cat', 'cat', 'fox', 'lion', 'cat']

In the above example, the statement 2 indicates that the item tiger should be inserted at the index 0. Hence it is appended at the first location of the list.

4.2.7. Remove Method

The remove method is used for removing the first occurrence of the element on the list. The example is shown below

Example 8

#Remove Method Implementation

```
ab=['cat','rat','cat','cat','fox','lion','cat'];
ab.insert(0,"Tiger");
print(ab)
ab.remove("cat")
print(ab)
```

Output:

['Tiger', *'cat',* 'rat', 'cat', 'cat', 'fox', 'lion', 'cat']

['Tiger', 'rat', 'cat', 'cat', 'fox', 'lion', 'cat']

In the above example, the first occurrence of item cat is removed from the list using the remove method.

4.2.8. Pop Method

The Pop method removes the indexed element. It takes index as the argument.

Example 9

#Pop Method Implementation

```
ab=['one','two','three','four'];
ab.pop(2)
print(ab)
```

Output:

['one', 'two', 'four']

The reason for the above output is due pop method argument takes the value 2. The list index is of

One	Two	**Three**	Four
0	1	**2**	3

Hence, the item 'Three' is removed from the list.

4.2.9. Reversing the list:

We can easily reverse the list using the reverse method. It uses the syntax, list_name.reverse().

Example 10
#Reverse Implementation
```
ab=['one','two','three','four'];
ab.pop(2)
print(ab)
ab.reverse()
print(ab)
```
Output:
```
['one', 'two', 'four']
['four', 'two', 'one']
```

4.2.10. Copying the list items

In order to copy the list items into another list as shallow copying process, we have to use copy operation. The following example will illustrates it,

Example 11
#Copy Implementation
```
ab=['one','two','three','four'];
ab.pop(2)
print(ab)
ab.reverse()
print(ab)
x=ab.copy()
print(x)
```
Output:
```
['one', 'two', 'four']
['four', 'two', 'one']
['four', 'two', 'one']
```

These are the various different operations on list. In the next section, let we discuss the data-structure called 'tuples'.

4.3. Tuples

Tuples are very similar to the list. But the only difference is that they are immutable (can't be changed), Hence we cannot able to perform the append and deletion operation with the tuples.

4.3.1 Creation of Tuples

The following syntax is used for creating the tuple.

Tuple_ Name= ('item1',........'item N');

The only deviation in the syntax is the usage of brackets.

Example 12

#Creation of Tuples

```
t1=('a','b','c')
print("tuple created!");
```

Output:

Tuple Created!

4.3.2. Operations on Tuples:

We can perform count and index operations with Tuples. It is similar to that of the methods in list (Refer Section: 4.2.5 – Count).

Can you answer?

1. Differentiate between tuples and list.

2. Write the Python program for creation of list of 10 flower names. Perform the following operations on it.

       (a) Sort the list

       (b) Add the flower to the end of the list

       (c) Add a flower at the index 4.

       (d) Count number of Jasmines in the list.

       (e) Pop some items from the list.

3. Is Tuples are immutable? What does it mean? Discuss.

4.4. Dictionary

As the name implies, dictionary holds the item along with its equivalent attribute. Consider the scenario in which the mark of a student to be stored along with the subject as Hindi $\rightarrow$ 30, English $\rightarrow$ 50, Physics $\rightarrow$ 40. At such cases, dictionary is used.

4.4.1. Creation of Dictionary

The creation of the dictionary follows the syntax given below,

       Dictionary_Name = {'Key' : 'Value', ...}

In our case, the subject name is the key and mark is the value.

Example 13
#Creation of Dictionary
     dicto={'Tamil':'20',
     'English' : '40',
     'Physics' : '35'}
     print ("Dictionary Created!");
Output:
     Dictionary Created!

4.4.2. Operations on Dictionary
4.4.2.1. Printing value for given key
     To print the value we have to pass the relevant key. It uses the syntax as *print dictionary _ name ['key']*. Let us consider the mark of Mr.John is stored in a dictionary named as John_dicto. At this case, if we want to know Mr.John's Physics mark we have to follow the following syntax,

Example 14
#Printing value for given key
     John_Dicto={'Tamil':'20',
     'English' : '40',
     'Physics' : '35'}
     print(John_Dicto['Physics'])
Output: 35
     Thus, we can easily get the value for the given key.

4.4.2.2. Adding Key – Pair Value:

In order to add the Key-Pair value into the dictionary, we have to use the following syntax, dictionary _ name ['key']=['val'];

Example 15
#Adding Key – Pair Value

```
John_Dicto={'Tamil':'20',
'English' : '40',
'Physics' : '35'}
print("Before Adding Key-Pair..")
print(John_Dicto)
John_Dicto['Chemistry']='45'
print("After Adding Key-Pair..")
print(John_Dicto)
```

Output:

Before Adding Key-Pair..
{'English': '40', 'Tamil': '20', 'Physics': '35'}
After Adding Key-Pair..
{'English': '40', 'Tamil': '20', 'Physics': '35', 'Chemistry': '45'}

4.4.2.3. Deleting a Key – Pair Value:

The following syntax will delete the Key – Pair value, for such operation we have to pass the key as the parameter not the value. The syntax is del dictionary _ name ['key'].

Example 16
#Deleting Key – Pair Value

John_Dicto={'Tamil':'20',
'English' : '40',
'Physics' : '35'}
    del John_Dicto['Tamil'];
    print(John_Dicto)

Output:
    {'English': '40', 'Physics': '35'}

4.4.2.4. Deleting all items in the dictionary:

To delete all Key – Pair values in the dictionary, we have to use the keyword clear. The syntax is of *dictionary _ name.clear()* which makes the dictionary to empty.

Example 17

#Deleting All Key – Pair Values
    John_Dicto={'Tamil':'20',
                'English' : '45'}
    John_Dicto.clear();
    print(John_Dicto);

Output:
    {}
#Empty Dictionary

4.4.2.5. Making shallow copy of dictionary

To make the shallow copy of the dictionary, we have to use the syntax as

   new_dictionary_name =
   old_dictionary_name.copy()

which will copy the content of the old dictionary to the new dictionary.

Example 18

#Making Shallow Copy of Dictionary
     John_Dicto={'Tamil':'20',
              'English' : '45'}
     John_Dicto001=John_Dicto.copy()
     print(John_Dicto001)
Output:
     {'Tamil':'20', 'English' : '45'}

4.4.3. Conversion of Dictionary to the List:

To perform conversion of Dictionary to list data-structure we have to use the following syntax,

     List_name = dictionary _ name.items()

Example 19

#Converting Dictionary to List
     John_Dicto={'Tamil':'20',
   'English' : '40',
   'Physics' : '35'}
     list001=John_Dicto.items()
     print(list001)

Output:
dict_items([
('Physics', '35'),
('Tamil', '20'),
 ('English', '40')])

Can you answer?
1. Explain various operations on dictionaries with suitable examples.

HARIPRASATH.P

2. Discuss the conversion of dictionary to list with example.

4.5. Sets

Set is a built – in data structure of Python which provides unordered collection of items whereas the list provides the ordered collection of items and tuples provides ordered collection of items in immutable format.

4.5.1. Creation of Set

The creation of set uses the syntax,

Set_Name = set (['item 1', 'item 2' ...... 'item N'])

Example 20

#Creation of Set

```
set1=set(['car',
'bike',
'van',
'lorry'
'train'
])
print("Set Created!");
```

Output:

Set Created!

4.5.2. Operations on Set

4.5.2.1. Adding an Item into a set:

Syntax : set_name.add('item');

Example 21

#Adding Item into a set

```
set1=set(['car',
'bike',
'van',
'lorry'
'train'
])
set1.add('aeroplane')
print(set1)
```

Output

{'van', 'car', 'lorrytrain', 'bike','aeroplane'}

Thus we can easily add the items into a set.

4.5.2.2. Clearing the set

Syntax : set_name.clear()

Example 22   ***#Clearing the set***

```
set1=set(['car',
'bike',
'van',
'lorry'
'train'
])
set1.clear()
```

Output: ([])

4.5.2.3. Discard Operation

The discard operation is used for removing an item from the set. The item which is passed as the parameter to the discard method will gets removed from the set. The syntax is set_name.discard('item_name')

Example 23

#Discard Operation

```
set1=set(['car',
'bike',
'van',
'lorry'
'train'
])
set1.discard('bike')
print(set1)
```

Output

{'van', 'car', 'lorrytrain'}

4.5.2.4. Difference Operation

The set difference operation is used for taking the difference (*A* – *B*) operation between two sets *A and B*. If there exist sets A and B, then the difference operation will produce the resultant *as A* – *B*. The set difference operation will remove the same elements from the two sets. The syntax is set_name1.difference(set_name2)

Example 24
#Set Difference Operation

```
set1=set(['car',
'bike',
'van',
'lorry'
'train'
])
set2=set(['train'
'lorry'
'bus'
'scooty'
])
print(set1.difference(set2))
```

Output:

{'bike', 'van', 'car', 'lorrytrain'}

4.5.2.5. Set Intersection Operation

The set intersection will returns the same (common) elements that are available in both sets. If set A has {x,y,z} and set B has {m,n,o,p,q,r,s,t,u,v,w,x} then set intersection of A and B returns the common element {x} as result. The syntax of set intersection is *set1. intersection(set2)*.

Example 25
#Set Intersection Operation

```
set1=set(['car',
```

```
'bike',
'van',
'lorry'
'train'
])
set2=set(['car',
'lorry',
'bus',
'scooty',
])
print(set1.intersection(set2))
```

Output:
```
{car}
```

4.5.2.6. Set – Difference Update

This operation will removes element that are exists in set B from set A. the syntax is setA.difference_update(setB).

Example 26

#Set Difference Update
```
set1=set(['car',
'bike',
'van',
'lorry',
'train'
])
set2=set(['car',
'lorry',
'bus',
```

```
'scooty',
])
set1.difference_update(set2)
print(set1)
```

Output:

```
{'train', 'van', 'bike'}
```

4.5.2.7. Set Disjoint

This function returns true value if there is no intersection operation. It uses the syntax set1.isdisjoint(set2).

4.5.2.8. Set Union

The Set Union operation will takes the union of two sets. i.e., it will concatenate the elements of set without duplication. The syntax is of set1.union(set2).

Example 27
#Set Union Operation

```
set1=set(['car',
'bike',
'van',
'lorry',
'train'
])
set2=set(['car',
'lorry',
'bus',
'scooty',
```

])
        print(set1.union(set2))
Output:
        {'van', 'bike', 'bus', 'train', 'car', 'lorry',
'scooty'}

4.5.2.9. Pop Operation

In list the pop will remove the indexed element whereas in sets, the pop operation will removes the last element from the set. It uses the syntax set_name.pop().

Can you answer?

1. Discuss various operations on sets.

2. Create two sets A and B which holds the Toppers name of two subjects namely Physics and Chemistry. Hence perform the following operations

(i) Identify the Toppers who are in both subjects.

(ii) Identify the unique toppers of Physics

(iii) Generate overall Topper's set.

(iv) Remove the last candidate from the Physics topper set.

3. Explain set difference and set-intersection with suitable example.

4. What is the difference between pop operations on list and set?

5. Print ([]) on the console using the built-in data structure.

HARIPRASATH.P

PRACTICE CORNER!
Test – 01

Some of the Python codes from the text-book are shown below re-write them as indentation oriented. Hence, predict the output of it.

```
1. t=1
x=2
t=t+1
print(t)
print("T")
print(x)
print(X)
```

```
2. x=(2+3)*(2-3)+(2/4)
y=(5/2)+(8*(5-4)+(4/3))
z=(9+5-(2+9)+4*(4/2))
k=x*(x+1)-y*(y-1)+z*(z-1)
print(x," ",y," ",z," ",k)
```

```
3. X= "2.455"
print(type(X))
```

```
4. def add(a,b):
c=a+b;
print("Addition Result",c)
def sub(a,b):
c=a-b;
```

```python
print("Subtraction Result",c)
def mul(a,b):
c=a*b;
print("Multiplication Result",c)
print("Enter your choice 1.Addition 2.Subtraction
3. Multiplication ");
ch=int(input());
if(ch==1):
a=int(input("Enter A value"));
b=int(input("Enter B value"));
add(a,b)
elif(ch==2):
a=int(input("Enter A value"));
b=int(input("Enter B value"));
sub(a,b)
elif(ch==3):
a=int(input("Enter A value"));
b=int(input("Enter B value"));
mul(a,b)
else:
print("Invalid Choice");
```

5. X= 2
Y= 5
```python
print(X>Y) #Greater than Operator
print(X)
 print(X<=Y) #Less than or equal to Operator
print(X>=Y) #Greater than or equal to Operator
print(X==Y) #equal to operator
```

```
print(X!=Y) #Not equal to operator

6. Print("Hey");

7. print (r " Hello Hey How are you?");

8. T= "COSMIC RAYS"
print(T.title());

9. v1=int(input("Enter the First Operand"))
v2=int(input("Enter the Second Operand"))
print("1 - Addition 2 - Subtraction 3 -
Multiplication 4 - Division ")
v3=int(input("Enter the Operator"))
if(v3==1):
print(v1+v2)
elif(v3==2):
print(v1-v2)
elif(v3==3):
print(v1*v2)
elif(v4==4):
print(v1/v2)
else:
print("Check your Input! Operator Incorrect!");

10. def k(c,a=1,b=2):
return(a+b+c);
x=k(4) print(x);
```

Test – 02

Some of the Python codes from the text-book are shown below re-write them as indentation oriented. Hence, predict the output of it.

1. X="chemistry in action";
print(X.isdecimal())
print(X.isnumeric())
print(X.isalpha())
print(X.isdigit())
print(X.islower())
print(X.isidentifier())

2. t=1
x=2
t=t+1
print(t)
print("T")
print(x)
print(X)

3. v1=int(input("Enter the First Operand"))
v2=int(input("Enter the Second Operand"))
print("1 - Addition 2 - Subtraction 3 -
Multiplication 4 - Division ")
v3=int(input("Enter the Operator"))
if(v3==1):
print(v1+v2)

HARIPRASATH.P

```python
elif(v3==2):
print(v1-v2)
elif(v3==3):
print(v1*v2)
elif(v4==4):
print(v1/v2)
else:
print("Check your Input! Operator Incorrect!");
```

```python
4. X=5
Y=24
print(X>>Y)
print(Y<<Y)
```

```python
5. print("\t");
print("'Hi! Hello'");
print("a");
```

```python
6. def f1(a):
a=a+1;
print(a)
a=a-1;
print(a)
a=a*1;
print(a)
print("End of Function f1");
def f2(b):
b=b+2;
print(b)
```

```
b=b-2;
print(b)
b=b*2;
print(b)
f1(5)
f2(10)

7. a=2;
if a==2:
print ("hi");

8. X=3
Y=4.22
Z=3+4j
M= "member"
print(type(X))
print(type(Y))
print(type(Z))
print(type(M))

9. def add(a,b=3):
c=a+b;
print("Addition Result",c)
def sub(a,b=4):
c=a-b;
print("Subtraction Result",c)
def mul(a,b=5):
c=a*b;
print("Multiplication Result",c)
```

```python
print("Enter your choice 1.Addition 2.Subtraction
3. Multiplication ");
ch=int(input());
if(ch==1):
a=int(input("Enter A value"));
add(a)
elif(ch==2):
a=int(input("Enter A value"));
sub(a)
elif(ch==3):
a=int(input("Enter A value"));
mul(a)
else:
print("Invalid Choice");
```

10. #Translation Table Creation
```python
X= "ABC"
Y= "123"
Z=maketrans(X,Y);
```

```python
#Translation Operation
q= "A for Apple, B for Ball, C for Cat";
print(q.translate(Z));
```

Test – 03

Some of the Python codes from the text-book are shown below re-write them as indentation oriented. Hence, predict the output of it.

```
1. a=1;
b=2;
print ("b");
if(b==0):
print("Good Day");
```

```
2. print("Enter your age")
age=input();
print("Your age is"+age);
```

```
3. def pas():
pass #Empty Function
pas()
```

```
4. X=3
Y=4.22
Z=3+4j
M= "member"
print(type(X))
print(type(Y))
print(type(Z))
print(type(M))
```

5. y= "binomial theorem";
print(len(Y));

6. X=5
Y=2
print(X&Y) #Bitwise AND Operation
print(X|Y) #Bitwise OR Operation
print(X^Y) #Bitwise XOR Operation
print(~Y) #Invert Operation

7. print ("Enter A")
a=int(input())
print ("Enter B")
b=int(input())
c=(a+b)*(a+b)
d=(a*a)+(b*b)+(2*a*b)
print("L.H.S",+c)
print("R.H.S",+d)

8. X= "car"
print(len(X))

9. T= "COSMIC RAYS"
print(T.title());

10. Y= "one space"
print(len(Y));

——————.

Test yourself – 01

1. (a) List the advantages of Python.
   (b)Deepa wants to perform subtract the two complex numbers 2 + 4j   and 4 + 9j. Write the Python code to perform so.

2. (a) Explain how it works?

   for i in range(1,4):

   (b) Reason out the cause of the error in the following code:

   ```
   assert=1
   assert=assert+6;
   print(assert);
   ```

3. (a) Write the Python code for finding cube root and square root of the user given input number.
   (b) Compare the differences between single and multi-line comment.

4. (a) Write Python code for multiplication tabulation.
   (b) Derive the Python code for simple login form.

5.   (a) Classify: Programming languages.
       (b) What are pre-defined functions? Explain the followings:
              (a) range()
              (b) len()
              (c) type()

6.   (a) List any five keywords.
       (b) Write the Python code for finding cube root and square root of the user given input number.

7.   (a) What will be the output of len() function in the following cases?

       (1) "EXPLAIN"
       (2) "Suffering from"
       (3) "tentative examination"

       (b) When to use continue? Discuss.

8.   (a) Get two numbers from the user and display on the console using Python.
       (b) Give the syntax of Capitalize function.

9.   (a) State the reason for the output of len("New Year"); is 8.
       (b) What happens if you press Ctrl + D and Ctrl + C if you are in Python IDLE?

HARIPRASATH.P

10. (a) Write Python code for implementing
     (a) break
     (b) pass
     (c) return

   (b) Write a Python code for finding the string entered is palindrome or not using string functions.
   _____.

HARIPRASATH.P

www.ingramcontent.com/pod-product-compliance
Lightning Source LLC
Chambersburg PA
CBHW071426050326
40689CB00010B/1998